Country Boy's Tales

Of a

Simpler Time

This book is dedicated to all of those people
included in each story. Without their impact on
our lives, there would be no stories. Our lives are
better for knowing each of them and we hope they
remember us as fondly as we do them.

My name is James (Jim) Ferguson. I was born and raised in southeast Missouri in a place and time when things were simpler, where people didn't lock the doors at night, and where kids could be kids. As a young boy I would often rise with the sun and leave home--whether by stick horse or bicycle--seeking adventure. I spent many a day fishing and hunting on the numerous drainage ditches around my home or collecting Indian relics from the hundreds of Indian mounds scattered throughout southeast Missouri.

I attended school at Gideon Elementary and High School which is where I met Terry Weldon. We played baseball together and kicked around the streets of Gideon on occasions. Although our adult lives took separate paths, we have now reunited and have written our life stories and combined them into this book. Perhaps this glimpse into our lives will awaken some of the memories of your lives and put a smile upon your face. I hope you enjoy these stories.

# # #

My name is Terry L. Weldon. I was born at home
between Gideon and Malden Missouri. I was four
years old and lived with my grandparents when my
mother passed away. I lived with them until I was
eighteen. I left home like most to find my fame and
fortune. After trying several jobs, I married Colette
Gregory, as of June 2012, we've been together forty
two years, we've had three children, who's had
seven grandchildren. I joined the United States Air
Force in 1974 and retired in 1994. The older I get, the
more I reflect to my years back in the Bootheel of
Missouri where my value system was established. I
am a firm believer in family values and think the
family unit is the backbone of our society. I feel the
disassembly of the family unit directly contributes to
the disassembly of our moral structure. I Can't make
my children and grandchildren their kids the way I
raised mine, however, through reading these simple
stories, maybe they will decide to instill some of
these values in their children.

COWBOYS AND STICK HORSES

By: Jim Ferguson

If you are fifty-five or older, you should remember the first televisions and the shows that were on. The reception wasn't that good; more often than not the picture was "snowy" requiring someone in the family forever having to go out and turn the antenna. It was also very common to loose the station halfway through a show. Everything was black and white, there was no color. We definitely did not have flat screens or digital television, but it was still great entertainment. Some of the most popular shows to watch were *"Hop Along Cassidy," "Gun Smoke,"* and *"Have Gun Will Travel."* We also had the singing cowboys: Roy Rogers, Gene Autry, and several other popular crooners. Of course, Saturday morning favorites included The Lone Ranger and Tonto, Wild Bill Hickok (remember Jingles, his sidekick, always lagging behind and shouting "Wait for Me Wild Bill?"). Roy Rogers and Dale Evans also had a Saturday morning show and always sang *"Happy Trails to You"* at the end of each show. There was also *"Fury," "My Friend Flicka,"* and *"The Rifle Man"*. And then there was Sky King, a rancher who flew a plane.

Now being a young boy during that era there were a few thing you just had to have such as a gun and holster. One Christmas I remember getting a new gun and holster and not just any gun/holster but a Lone Ranger gun with pearl handles. It also shot silver bullets. I'm guessing the bullets were spring loaded by the way they would shoot across the living room. Gee, you sure couldn't buy one like that for a four year old today--people would say it is child endangerment.

Not to mention that I got a Daisy BB gun for Christmas by the time I was six. In fact, my oldest sister and I got a pair of them the same year. Hers was blue, and mine was brown. Many a sparrow met their fate because of those two BB guns. I also have a friend who carries a scar right between his eyes to this day as a result of telling my brother that he didn't have the nerve to shoot him. Not a very smart thing to do. When you throw down a challenge, be prepared for the results.

Now the other thing you had to have was a horse. Now as much as I wanted a real horse, I never got one as a kid. I did later in life which was a big mistake and a whole different story. However, there wasn't a kid around who had any more fun with a real horse than I did with my stick horse. A stick horse is nothing more than a broom handle cut off with a hole drilled into one end of it so you could attach reins to it. (Now by the time my boys were old enough for a stick horse you could buy one with the likeness of a horse's head attached to it.) Living on the farm as I did growing up, I had hundreds of acres to ride my trusted steed and ride him I did! Riding a stick horse isn't as easy as just jumping on and running off down the road or across the field. You had to develop your gait; otherwise you would get your feet tangled up with the stick and be "thrown." Owning a gun and holster set as well as a good stick horse, you had the two main things you needed to be a cowboy. But if you really wanted to be decked out, you could talk your dad out of one of his handkerchiefs. Ah, they made a fine neckerchief and also a great mask if you wanted to rob a stage coach or a train. If you were pretending to be on a cattle drive they would help keep the dust out of your mouth. The last three things a boy needs in order to be a top notch cowboy are a good pair of gloves, a pair of boots, and a cowboy hat. Now boots were optional. We all went barefooted then anyways so you could do without them but...they would have been nice to have. A pair of gloves was nice, too. I remember getting a pair for Christmas once that had large cuffs with fringe on them. There are not many things in life that I was more proud of than those gloves. Last but not least was a cowboy hat. The hat was a must have. It didn't have to be fancy. No, just an old felt hat would do--one that would serve to shade the eyes, or hold water so you could water your horse and, on occasion, putting black berries in it would be fine. As a young boy I rode that stick horse with my six-shooter on my side with my neckerchief, gloves, and hat many a day catching horse thieves, cattle rustlers, bank robbers, and occasionally chasing down a run-away stage coach and saving the lives of the women onboard. But as with all things, time changes. Tying my faithful steed to the post of the porch one evening as I always did, I did not know then it would be for the last time. The next morning instead of mounting up on the stick horse, I walked over to the bicycle that was leaned up against the porch and discovering I could go further and faster, I rode away looking for new adventures.

Great Memories.

I'M THE BEST

By: Terry Weldon

I heard a song the other day that took me back to my childhood more than any other.

When I was a little boy living with my grandparents after all of their children had grown up and moved away from home I would stand in our driveway and bat rocks to the opposite side of the road. Oddly enough, we never ran out of rocks.

I didn't actually have a real bat, usually a broom handle that was "accidently" broken on the four by four post on the back porch! Another odd thing was every time I needed a new bat, a broom handle came up broken, I never did figure that out. Reckon Granny Beasley did?

It was almost sunset and there were no stadium lights. We were always in the world series. I would play both teams and announce the game at the same time.

So here I was, the greatest batter in the world, standing at home plate, 9th inning, two outs, bases loaded, we were down three to nothing.

As I hear the crowd roar for the first pitch, I toss the rock into the air and swing with all I've got, The rock drops to the ground. Strike one!

I wasn't shaken by that one and I prepare for the next pitch. Again the crowd is even louder than before as I toss the rock into the air and focus as hard as I can. I have batted over ten thousand rocks all the way across the road many times in the past and this was no different. Again the rock hits the ground. Strike Two!

I did not flinch as I removed my baseball cap and wiped the sweat from my brow. I stood there for a moment with my eyes closed and listened to the crowd cheering me on. I knew I was the greatest batter of all times as I tossed the rock into the air. Everything was happening in slow motion at this point and I knew this was it, I could imagine the rock flying all the way to the road ditch across the highline wires. But, the rock hits the ground. Strike three! My Granny called me into the house for supper and as I walked down the driveway to our back porch, I thought to myself; I never knew I could pitch like that...

A FORBIDDEN LOVE

By: Jim Ferguson

Those of you who have read the stories I've previously written know they have been about the things I've done in my life either as a young boy or my hunting and fishing adventures as I grew older or they were about someone in my life who meant a lot to me. I would now like to tell you a story that was told to me many years ago--a story that I have never told anyone. As a young boy I was forever traveling around the countryside looking for Indian relics. I was either walking or riding a bicycle often being several miles away from home. On my travels there were several houses scattered about the farmlands of southeast Missouri where I would stop and get myself a drink of water from the water hose that always stay hooked up to the pump outside. On one of the trips as I approached the house to get a drink, I noticed the lady who lived there was sitting in a swing on the porch. When I asked her if it would be alright if I got myself a drink from the hose she said she could do better than that. She said if I would come and sit for a while she would fix me a glass of iced tea. As I set on the steps she returned with the tea and handed it to me. She sat back in the swing and said nothing for a few moments but just stared into the sunset. I finally asked her if there was something wrong. She turned my way and said, "Today I went to the funeral of the man I have loved all my life." Now I knew this woman and had always been told her husband had died several years ago. Now I was confused and told her so. For the next hour or so I sat on the steps of her house and listened to the story she told me.

It began when she was in her late teens--a time when she should have been dating and she did some. However there was always this man in her heart. The problem was he was at least ten years her senior and was married with children. Why she felt the way she did about him she didn't know. Maybe it was the way he always spoke to her always asking how she was doing, but never saying anything out of the way to her. But she could sense that there was something between them. It also seemed that whenever there were functions of the church, school, or community, they would end up talking for hours but they were never alone. They were always amongst others. The lady told me this went on for months. Finally she had a chance to talk to him alone and she informed him of her feelings. To her dismay he said she was just young and, in time, would fall in love with someone her age and she would look back upon this time and wonder what she was ever thinking. He said he knew this to be true because she was a very beautiful lady and would have men knocking at her door frequently. However she knew in her heart that it was love. As the years passed, she would continue to see him in the community with his daughters and would often stop to chat. Nothing was ever said about the talk they had that day. In due time she also married and had children of her own. Unfortunately her marriage wasn't a good one. Although her husband became very abusive, she stayed with him thinking it would be best for the children.   As time passed she and her husband moved away. The abuse became so bad she planned to divorce him, but he died before she could divorce him. This allowed her to live a happier life. She worked to provide for herself and her daughters always keeping the memory of her true love in her mind--a love that had been forbidden to her. But little did she know that time has a way of changing all things.

On a return trip to her hometown years later as fate would have it she met the man of her dreams. She was once again dismayed to learn that his wife had died a couple years earlier and that he had just recently remarried. He mentioned that he had often thought of her and wondered where she was and how she was doing.   Since he had no way of knowing she was widowed, he naturally assumed she was happily married and resisted trying to find her. After all, it had been close to twenty years since the night of their talk. They talked for over an hour.

He promised her that if there were ever any more changes in his life in the future, he would get in touch with her. He kissed her on the cheek and they went their separate ways--this time both knowing that there was more than just a fondness for each other but also knowing what they felt was forbidden.

As she continued to sit on the porch she told me that during the next ten years she would occasionally receive a letter from him inquiring as to her wellbeing or she would make a trip back to her home town and would often see him at the local coffee shop and chat with him and the other locals who gathered there for their morning coffee. As she continued to tell me this story, I could sometimes see a tear gather in her eyes. She said she moved back to this town after she retired from thirty years doing factory work in the city. By this time she was pushing sixty years of age and he was already seventy. His health was beginning to fail and his wife was very frail and demanded all of his time. With the exception of a few telephone calls and a few meetings in town, their love was never allowed to bloom. I asked her why he never divorced his wife and married her. She replied, "Oh, no, we never could have done that. It wouldn't have been right. Of course I would have married him if things had been different; but sometimes in life it is enough knowing that you are loved by the one you love. And, for us it was."

As I left the house that day and headed home I pondered on the lady's story. Although I was young I knew life could be disappointing sometimes but to love someone your whole life like she did and never being able to be with them must be one of the worst things in life even if it is "A Forbidden Love."

Thanks for the memories, Ma'am.

I still remember your story.

A SUMMER AT GRANNY'S

By: Jim Ferguson

For the last few weeks I've been looking back at my life and writing short stories of the things I've done and the situations in which I have found myself. Most of the stories have been about fishing or hunting trips with friends and family. During this reflection process, it has taken me back to my childhood and to a fond memory of the time I spent a week or so with my grandparents who lived in the small town of Wilburn, Arkansas in the foothills of the Ozarks.

If you visited that part of Arkansas in the mid-to-late fifties, it was like stepping back it time. My grandpaw ran an old country store and a blacksmith shop. The people came to their store in wagons drawn by teams of horses or mules. There was a hitching rail in front of the store for tying up the team as well as a whittler's bench in front for the men to sit and talk or whittle. To this day I still have a short piece of chain carved out of cedar wood made by my grandpaw while he was sitting on that bench. My grandpaw was a one-legged man having lost a leg in midlife from a spider bite. Since he was not at all pleased with the fit of the artificial leg he was given and since he was a blacksmith, he carved himself a leg out of a piece of wood while he sat on that bench. He also fashioned the hardware to make it fit his leg in the ole black smith shop. Nothing more than a peg leg just like the ones worn by pirates in the movies. He wore that old peg leg for the rest of his life or, rather, until he got where he couldn't get around anymore. He spent the last few years of the eighty-seven that he lived in bed. My mother still has her daddy's peg leg.

Many an hour I spent with my grandpaw in the ole blacksmith shop. I would turn the handle on the blower that kept the fire hot in the forge while he hammered out horseshoes or plow points by hand, heating them up and shaping them on his anvil. Even now I can still picture in my mind that old forge and hear him saying, "Crank that handle, boy."

The farm where the house and store sat was about thirty acres and we kids had free run of the place. There were creeks and springs for wading and catching tadpoles. There was also a slate hill that we played on using an old car hood as a sled. Great times and great memories were made there.

Now as most of my memories show, I've gotten myself into some fix or trouble. Why should this one be any different? This particular time involves one of my sisters and a couple of cousins. Being girls, they were out front one day making mud pies. Why girls do this is beyond me--unless they are practicing their cooking skills. I was not at all interested in making mud pies and I didn't take up cooking for another forty years. On the other hand, I did think it would be appropriate to see how they tasted and I began to feed one of my cousins the mud pie she made. Upon hearing the screaming and crying, my granny came out and threatened me telling me to get away and leave the girls alone. Fearing my granny's wrath, I went on my way looking for some other form of entertainment. I soon discovered my granny had put new plastic on the windows in preparation for the winter (to help keep the cold wind from blowing in through the drafty windows). I soon learned if I took my finger and pushed, it would pop a hole in the plastic and make a sound similar to the bubble packs we all love to play with today. Observing me do this, my cousins and my sister must have decided that I didn't get the beating I deserved over the mud pies, so they went and told Granny on me. Here she came--this time carrying a switch. Now having been down that road before in my life, I decided it was time for me to leave and I ran. When Granny ordered me to come back, I shouted over my shoulder that she couldn't catch me and off I went down the hill to the creek where I spent the rest of the afternoon playing until time to come in for the night. Now upon returning to the house that night I learned a very important lesson of life. You may run and you may hide, but unless you can live on your own, you have to come home some time. When dealing with Granny that meant the punishment is there waiting for you when you do come home.

Now as the years passed Granny and Grandpaw got older and were in bad health. As a result, they moved in with us when I was in my teenage years. This story was often repeated jokingly by Granny when I was doing something: "Remember you have to come home some time."

During the years they lived with us, I spent many hours sitting beside Grandpaw and cutting his twist tobacco so he could smoke it in his pipe, listening to his stories, and hearing him sing his old songs. Here is one of our old favorites he would often sing to the tune of "At the Cross."

> At the bar, at the bar where I smoked my first cigar as the money from my pockets rolled away. It was there by chance that I tore my Sunday pants and now I'm wearing them every day.

Grandpaw died at the age of 87 in 1968 which is the year I turned sixteen. Granny lived to be 103 years old and died in 1997.

In memory of Granny and Grandpaw.

WITCH ON RIDDLE HILL

By: Terry Weldon

Everyone knew there was a witch living on Riddle Hill, just West of Malden Missouri. She had around twenty five dogs and lived on a gravel road. We would drive by slowly and yell to get the dogs riled up. They would chase us about fifty yards and turn around and head back to the house. We would go down the road and turn around to do it again. This was fun for teenage boys in the 1960s.

One night near Halloween we took a spin up to pester the old witch on Riddle Hill. I don't remember who all was there, but I think there were four of us. I know we were in Dennis Skidmore's pickup truck and I think it was Kent Reynolds, Ronnie Lowery and I. When we turn off "J" highway I told Dennis to let me get in the back of the truck. He was more than happy to let me do that. I had two cans of lighter fluid and I told him to drive slowly and I would spray the lighter fluid on the gravel road and light it so we could see the dogs as they chased us. He slowed down to about five miles per hour; I sprayed the lighter fluid and stepped over the tailgate of his truck to the bumper, holding the tailgate with my left hand I leaned over as far as I could. (I didn't want to burn the truck up), I wasn't stupid you know. I lit the lighter fluid and it worked just like I thought. The road lit up like day time, and here came the dogs, just as they left the yard Dennis hit the gas and there I went, right in the middle of the road, all lit up, so every dog could see me good. This didn't look good. I scrambled to my feet and headed for the truck full speed, looking back to see if the dogs were gaining on me. At the same time Dennis slowed down and BAM, right into the tailgate of the truck I ran, almost knocked me out. Dennis heard me hit and thought I had jumped back into the bed of the truck, so he took off. There I was, again with the dogs bearing down on me. Once I came to my senses, I left the dogs behind and this time, I cleared the tailgate of the truck and landed up against the cab. We got away from them and turned around for one for more pass at the witches' house. This time the lighter fluid had burned out and it was pitch black. Dennis decided to slow down again, after all, they were in the safety of the cab of the truck and I was standing in the back with one leg over the tailgate standing on the bumper. I was laughing and yelling when the witch came out of the house with what looked like a cannon. Dennis didn't see the witch come out of her house and he stopped the truck to let the dogs get a good taste of me! I had eight or ten dogs about twenty feet from me hanging on the bumper, screaming get out of here, she's got a shotgun. When he saw her coming up to the road, he hit the gas again, and again, onto the road I went. This was it, I was a goner. The barrels on that double-barreled shotgun looked like a ten gauge. For those of you that don't know what that means. The barrel was about the size of a can of store bought biscuits. At least they looked that big to me. I scrambled to my feet and this time I ran on ahead of the truck and waited for them to pick me up. Not really, he stopped again and just as I landed in the bed of the truck, the buckshot sprayed the back of the truck. We drove away screaming and laughing. What a night that was, however, it seems to stand out in the memories of the guys in the cab of the truck more than the one in the bed of the truck. For you teenagers living in and around Gideon and Malden, take a drive out there, I bet money, the Witch of Riddle Hill is still out there...

AND THE ICE CRACKED

By: Jim Ferguson

It is cold outside and snowing hard. The national weather service has just issued a blizzard warning and urged people to stay inside except in case of emergency. My kind of weather! I went outside and fired my ole truck up trying to get the snow melted off the windshield, which will take a long time. The old heater in the '65 Ford just does not do a whole lot of good but it is what it is. So while it is doing its thing, I have time to get my stuff together: gun, shells, toboggan, coat, and gloves. My goal and aim today is to enjoy the huge snow we are having. The game will be holed up in their dens which makes it a good time to catch rabbits sitting. Plus, with the ditches frozen, I'll have a good chance of catching a lot of ducks sitting on whatever water that may still be open.

After getting everything in the cab of the truck and the snow melted off the best it's going to melt, I've headed out. My first stop will be the floodway ditches. Since it was pointed out to me in another story that I was telling, not everyone knows what or where the floodway ditches are, I'll explain. They are canals that were dug through the bootheel of Missouri back years ago to drain the swamp resulting in southeast Missouri becoming some of the best farmland in the world.

Ha! This weather is just what I've been waiting for. There are two reasons that I love this type of weather. Number one: it is good, crisp hunting weather. Number two: most people are laid up in their homes just riding out the storm and that includes the game wardens. And that is a good thing. Not that I plan on breaking any big game laws. It's just that I look at things a little differently than they do. For instance, a person is allowed four ducks a day. If a guy (or gal) hunts every day, they would be allowed 28 ducks per week. However, I don't get to hunt every day so if I kill 28 in one day, I am still within the limit for the week. Do you see my reasoning?

I've now spent over an hour hunting on Jones' ditch which is the first of the four main floodway ditches between Gideon and Portageville. I've been hunting about two miles north of the bridges. I have managed to kill three rabbits--caught two of them sitting in their burrows while the third one jumped up a few yards in front of me. Unfortunately for him, in this deep snow he couldn't get away fast enough. The best is yet to come I think. I am working my way across the ditches and quite glad the water is frozen because I would hate to get wet today. I've been watching a ton of ducks going down in the third ditch over there which makes me think there must be an open hole of water in the ice somewhere. I have seen a time when a hole of water like that will fill full of ducks. I'm hoping that is the case today because it is still snowing like crazy and it's freezing cold. I now have ice frozen all over my beard. Burr!! I love it!

Upon reaching the crest of the berm between the second and third ditches, I spotted what I was looking for. There is a hole of open water maybe a hundred yards up the ditch. I'd guess maybe a 40 to 50 foot circle and from the looks of it you couldn't throw another duck in it. Backing down the berm, I removed the plug from my gun. Fully loading it, I began my stalk of the ducks. Now to make this a successful hunt, I need to slip close enough to them without spooking them before I'm in position. (It's not going to be easy since the snow is waste deep in places due to the drifting. In addition, the ground under the snow is overgrown with vines and bushes.)

Wow…I'm tired but I'm here. Only a few more feet to go. I'll take a minute to catch my breath. As of yet no ducks have left. In fact, I've noticed a few more have piled into the hole. THERE ARE A LOT OF DUCKS IN THAT HOLE. After making the last few feet I stood up, aimed, and fired all five shots into the hole. After reloading and shooting the cripples, I now have dead ducks all over the place. Finding a long stick with a fork on the end of it, I proceed out onto the ice to start retrieving my ducks. I pick up the dead ones that are on the ice and toss them to the bank. I use the stick to flip the ones in the water up on the ice. I was almost through and then it happened. I HEARD it first! It sounded like a .22 shell cracking through the air. Now for those of you who have ever watched the cartoon "The Road Runner"--well the expression on my face was probably like that of the wily coyote when he realized that he had just done something stupid. Like I said, I heard it first and then my world came apart. The ice on which I was standing broke! I was now in chest-deep water and it was so cold. This could get serious really quickly. Luckily, it wasn't over my head and I was able to bust the ice with the butt of my gun and wade to shallow water. Once there I was able to climb back up onto the ice and make it to the bank. However, I was still in trouble because I was a half-mile or better from my truck and six miles from town. After taking off my shoes to drain the freezing water from them, I removed the shoelaces, tied all the ducks together that I could, and looped them over my shoulders. I put the rest of them under my belt by their heads and necks. I headed across the ditches and toward the truck.

Goodness, it is cold! I do believe this is the coldest I have ever been in my life. I made it back to the truck and as I fired the truck up, I cussed myself for not getting this heater fixed. After raking the new-fallen snow off the windshield, I turned the truck around and headed for town. I am shaking and the roads are bad which means it's going to take a while to drive the six miles back to town. If I live through this, it's going to make one great memory when I get old, ha ha!

I've made it! I have just pulled into the driveway. Ice was breaking off my clothes as I got out and headed into the house. While I was stripping off my wet clothes, I asked my wife at the time to call my mother and ask her if she wanted to pluck some ducks. I headed to a tub of hot water.

I spent the rest of the afternoon in the tub warming up. And, yes, my mother did come over and pluck the ducks. As a matter of fact, she plucked enough feathers to make me a down-filled vest as well as a couple of feathered pillows. As I settled into bed that night I gave thanks to God for getting me back home alive and for blessing me with a GREAT DAY OF HUNTING AND A GREAT MEMORY!

BIG EDDIE

By: Terry Weldon

I was asked if I had any stories about my brother, Jack Weldon, which most of you all will remember as Puncho. Our family had a serious thing about everyone having a nickname. For example, Gladys, Patricia, Terry, Jerry, and Jack were called Peg, Sissie, Boy, Smokey, and Puncho. Seems like they could remember Jack as easily as Puncho? Anyway, Puncho was around eight or nine when our mom passed away in 1954. Our dad had left and was living in California at the time. I believe it was a year or so that he came back and took Puncho back to California with him to live. I didn't see him for several years, until he was around sixteen or seventeen and could drive himself back. When he would return to Missouri it was always a grand gathering. Everyone would gather to see what sort of young man he was growing into. He was always the cool kid from California.

After he was married, he decided to move and bring his family back to Malden, Missouri. With him came one of his friends named "Big Eddie". Eddie was what we Missouri Hillbillies would call the typical Californian, he was around six feet two inches, 300 pounds, with a long ponytail kept up with a rubber band. Way cool dude!

Eddie was fascinated by our Missouri culture so, Puncho and I decided to show him the ropes, first we took him out to show him one of the rights of passage for the young men around the bootheel of Missouri, "Stealing watermelons". It was a well known fact that all watermelon patch owners didn't care and that they could always give up three or four melons!

We also brought our wives who had never had this experience before. They would be the drivers for us, not that we needed to get away quickly, but you never knew when you might need to get back home, (in a hurry). We drove around just outside of Clarkton along a sandy ridge where the watermelons grew best until we found the perfect spot. Once we found it, we told the ladies to circle the block and pick us up in the very same place. Now, if you are from that are, you know the "blocks" are one mile square and it takes a while for someone who knew where they were going to get around, so two girls that had never been there before might take a little longer. And they were a little curious why we wanted them to drive with their headlights out until they got to the first turn and turn them off again when the rounded the last turn coming back. It was because we couldn't see the melons very well with the headlights in our eyes, yeah, that's it.

They were easing away while we briefed Big Eddie on how this system worked. We told him that it was very hard to tell the size of a watermelon while you were walking around in the patch, that it was much easier if you were crawling around, on your belly. Yeah, that's it.

Puncho and I could lay flatter that a spread-nanner (snake) if we had to, however, Big Eddie had a problem having a low profile. We crawled around a few minutes and all met back at the same spot as planned with two nice watermelons each. We sat up admiring each of our finds and looking for the girls when the first of many shotgun BBs rained down around us. I think we found the only farmer, that didn't have any watermelons to spare, and would like to have these six back. Puncho and I gave our four back immediately as we sprang to our feet and headed for the road ditch but Big Eddie wasn't about to give his up. That was fine with me; all I had to do was stay ahead of him. After the gunfire died down and we were all three lying in the road ditch wondering where the girls were with the car, Eddie decided that farmer was shooting at us. We told him it wasn't real bullets only salt rock he was shooting and it wouldn't sting very long. I also told Eddie, that the farmer couldn't shoot us after we made it to the road because the road wasn't his property, unless you were holding one of his watermelons! After the farmer reloaded and started shooting again, Puncho and I jumped into the car with the girls. We found Big Eddie down the road aways with one watermelon left. The next week Puncho and me took Big Eddie out "Stealing Pigeons", but that's another story.

BACK IN THE DAY

By: Jim Ferguson

For those of you who have been reading my stories, you are aware of some of the things I did in my youth for entertainment from corn cob fights to flying birds. It seems I was always able to come up with ways to entertain myself as did a lot of other kids who lived on the farms. As entertaining as they may appear to some of you, the things I did weren't really that unusual. Now I would like to tell you some of the stories my dad told me about the things they did back in his youth to entertain themselves. My dad was raised around Corning, Arkansas and was born in 1923. His mother died when he was twelve years old. Dad was the oldest of four children. He had two brothers (twins Ron and Don) and one sister Charlene. As far as entertainment goes, Dad and I enjoyed some of the same things in our youths. He fished and swam in Black River, went frogging, and hunted and trapped small game. I guess I got my love of hunting from him. However he did have a twist to his duck hunting. He told me they would set trot lines in the fields and bait them with corn (a trot line is a long line with several hooks tied to it for catching fish). In this case, the line was on dry ground so when the ducks came to feed in the fields they would swallow the hooks allowing Dad and his brothers to catch them. Certainly something the game warden would greatly frown on today. There were other forms of entertainment or mischief depending upon how a person looks at it in today's light. On Halloween they would go around the countryside taking wagons apart and reassembling them on the top of the barns of their neighbors. Of course, they would turn over or move outhouses--something that still went on in my youth as well. If you moved an outhouse in my day, you would always do it early in the evening of Halloween. Then you would hide and watch for the next bunch of boys to come through to turn it over hoping they would fall into the hole (funny but nasty). Another thing Dad always told us about is how they would take a five-gallon lard can and punch a small hole in the bottom. They would slide a string with a lot of resin on it back and forth through the hole creating a loud, eerie sound that could be heard for quite a distance. He always liked to set this up in the graveyard outside of town. I have always wanted to try this trick and may yet someday. My all-time favorite of Dad's stories was about the cow bell. Back in the thirties there were a lot more people who lived on small farms and raised chickens, hogs and always a milk cow to supply them with milk and butter. Instead of buying feed for the cattle, hogs, and chickens, folks raised it in small corn fields that were planted for that purpose. When the corn was gathered, it wasn't hauled to town to be but, rather, was put in the corn crib of the barn to feed the stock during the winter months. Now the way Dad told the story of the cow bell was this. He and his brothers would go late at night into the corn field of a neighbor. Separating they would take up different positions. One of them would start ringing the cow bell he carried with him. They would also grab an ear of corn and strip it off the stalk. When the farmer heard this noise, he would assume his milk cow was loose and was eating the corn. As the farmer got closer to the noise, my dad or his brother would stop ringing his bell and another one several yards away would start ringing his bell. They would repeat the process causing the farmer to change direction while continuing to look for the cow. Dad said they would do this several times then they would slip out of the field leaving the farmer thinking the cow must have made its way back to the barn. However Dad did say there were times when the farmer would be wise to their antics and come out of the house firing a shotgun over their heads. And as always, time passes and changes all things. There are very few outhouses to turn over any more; no more wagons to take apart; and no one keeps an ole mike cow around. Dad and both of his brothers have long passed and are no longer here to tell their stories. For those of us who have heard them, we thank them for the memories.

BUMBLEBEES AND ROCKS

By: Jim Ferguson

It's a shame that in today's world the kids are missing out on so much fun. Yes they have the latest technology with all the video and game boards. But if you were to take these things away, they would be lost; they don't know how to play.

Playing is an art and takes imagination. Why take a young baby, for instance. Give them a toy and what will they do? They will play with the box it came in, of course.

When I was young, we were lucky to get two or three toys for Christmas, and we usually had them broken or lost within a couple of months. Then we went back to the old true and proven means of entertainment. Now it just so happens my two favorites involved a stick or a wiffle ball bat if I was lucky. It included rocks and bumblebees. You could take those three things and have fun for hours. Now if you wanted to just have a leisurely day of hitting rocks, all you needed was a gravel road. It would supply you with all the marble-sized rocks you would need.

There are several different games you could play alone, but "rocks" was my favorite. This is how it was played. You would mark off the distance for first, second, third, and home bases with each base being further away. Now you took nine rocks and hit them thereby moving each runner around the bases according to the distance the rock was hit. After the nine rocks were hit, you changed batters. This was done by swapping from right to left handed to bat. And you continued through nine innings at which time the game was over. The advantage of this game was you could pretend to be any baseball player you wanted to be from Babe Ruth to Mickey Mantel. The game also helped build good hand-to-eye coordination. I contribute many base hits while playing baseball to the many hours I spent hitting rocks. Now there are some downsides to the game. If you weren't paying attention and allowed another kid to come within hearing distance, you could be laughed at for talking to yourself. The other problem was glass. Now I always played far from the house so I wouldn't break any windows. In fact, I liked hitting rocks around the barn area the best because there was an abundance of bumblebees there too. Even though I had been warned about breaking the windshield out of one of the farm trucks, it was still my favorite place to bat rocks. Now being the cautious type that I was, I always played with the big barn to my back--away from all the farm trucks and tractors. As I played one day, THE BASES WERE LOADED IN THE NINTH INNING WITH THE GAME TIED. HANK AARON WAS AT THE PLATE. SWING! FOUL BALL! You could also pretend to be Dizzy Dean, Peewee Reese, or Harry Carry and announce the game. Now this foul ball went high over the back stop (the barn) and, yep, it broke the back glass out of my dad's truck. The game was called due to tears.

Now bumblebees were a lot safer to hit than rocks at least as far as breaking glass. These bees I'm referring to are wood bees that make their homes in wood by boring a small, round hole into two-by-fours and two-by-sixes that framed the barn. Wood was one thing that we had plenty of. Now once again to play this game you needed a good stick or a wiffle ball bat. To play, you found a place where the bees had set up housekeeping and simply waited until they came out of the hole. You would wait until you could catch them hovering, then you took your swings. Now scoring was different than in the game of rocks. With bees it was how many you killed versus the numbers of times you were stung. Now this battle between the bees and me goes back to when I was really young--not more than four or five years of age. I remember standing on the back porch of our house near Hartzel about six miles northeast of Gideon. As I was standing there looking out toward the barn, I saw something flying toward me from the barn. Since I wasn't old enough to know what it was and wasn't fast enough to get out of the way, that ole bumblebee stung me right between the eyes. I couldn't see for days. From that day until now, the war still wages. Fifty-four or fifty-five years have passed since that day and here I am getting to be an old man, sitting on my cabin porch writing this story, when lo and behold I hear a bee buzzing. If I can find a good stick, I'll see if I still have what it takes to swat one...Strike One!

Great memories

CALVIN WALKER AND LILLIAN FRENCH

By: Jim Ferguson

I was born in Gideon, Missouri in 1952. Rumor has it that I came into this world screaming, kicking, and as hungry as a bear. I have no doubt about these rumors being true since my first experience in life was that of Dr. Hopkins holding me by my feet and slapping me on my naked butt. That is enough to make any new born scream and try to kick free. As far as being hungry, why shouldn't I be? My first food was milk delivered to me with a bottle and a rubber nipple stretched across it. Where were the fried potatoes and fried chicken I had heard the people talking about being so good the day before while sitting around the Sunday dinner table? After a day of rest, I was wrapped in a burlap sack and sent home with a woman whom I later discovered was my mother. We lived in the Gideon area and attended the Baptist Church at Tallapoosa until 1961. We then moved to Rose Dale, Mississippi where we stayed for one year before returning to Gideon where we attended the First Baptist Church. The First Baptist Church is where I became acquainted with the two people I would like to tell you a little about in this story--Calvin Walker and Lillian French. Calvin Walker worked for the postal service in Gideon and served as the music director at the church. But before I tell you about that part of his life, I would like to go back a few years and mention some earlier things. Calvin was a member of the "Greatest Generation." He served In the U.S. Army Air Corps during World War II and was attached to the 381st Air Group Eighth Army Air Corps stationed at Ridgewell, England. He flew thirty-two missions over Germany with his first mission being over Berlin. He was a radio operator and rear waste gunner. After the war Calvin returned to Gideon, married, and started raising a family. I'm not certain when Calvin began leading the music at First Baptist Church there in Gideon but he was leading it when we started going there in the early 60's. He had a strong baritone voice and sang at a lot of weddings in town and sang hundreds of solos throughout the years at church. Some of my favorite songs that I have heard Calvin sing are *"Heaven Came Down and Glory Filled My Soul," "He Touched Me,"* and *"O Holy Night."* My all-time favorite was *"How Great Thou Art."* I have heard a lot of religious singers in my life but I have **never** heard anyone who could sing this song better than Calvin Walker! If you didn't have goose bumps after hearing him sing this then, my friend, I'm afraid you don't have a religious bone in you. Calvin continued to be the music director at the church throughout the sixties and seventies and always conducted the choir for the Christmas and Easter cantatas. Although he retired as the music director in the early eighties, he continued to sing specials on occasional Sunday mornings. After he retired, I began leading the singing at the First Baptist Church; however, I will be the first to admit I wasn't even in the same class as Calvin. One thing in my life I always wanted to do--but never did---was to sing a special with Calvin. We frequently talked about it and even had a song prepared once but something came up and we never got around to it again. That is one of my regrets in life. It would have been an honor for me to be able to sing with Calvin.

There were a lot of people in our church that I looked up to. It would take a year to write stories about each and every one of them; however; I do want to take this time to mention one other person, Lillian French. Mrs. French was the janitor for the church as well as a cook for the school in Gideon. She also taught Sunday school. I don't think there was ever a child who attended her Sunday school classes on a regular basis who wasn't saved. An older lady, Mrs. French received respect from all who knew her and that respect that was well earned. She had a great sense of humor and loved baseball. If you wanted to get on her bad side and get a lecture, just say something bad about the St. Louis Cardinals. As time passed and we all grew older I continued to see Mrs. French and visit with her. Shortly after buying a Jeep in 1981, I was visiting Mrs. French when she informed me she had always wanted to go mudding in a Jeep. Since we had recently had a big rain, it was a good time to do just that. I helped Mrs. French into the Jeep and off to the floodways we went. Once there I was taking it easy not wanting to jar Mrs. French around. She told me she could have this much fun in anything but she wanted to do some mudding. So some mudding we did! By the time we got back to town you couldn't tell the color of the Jeep because it was covered with mud from one end to the other. She laughed and had a great time and I did as well. That was such special time with her that I will never forget it. And as always, time passes and changes all things. Neither Mrs. French nor Calvin Walker is here on this earth with us. Calvin lost his wife, Marilee, and I do believe he died mourning her loss. He truly loved her. Still to this day when I hear someone sing *"How Great Thou Art"* I always think of Calvin. Likewise, when I see a Jeep covered with mud I think of Mrs. French.

Thanks for the Memories.

YOU CAN TRUST ME

By: Terry Weldon

Around 1964, of my grandparent's children had left home except me and my Aunt Margie. My Aunt Margie and I became very close when I was around fourteen years old and up. Although I had one sister already, "Sissie", Margie was as close to a second sister as one can get. We were thick. I covered for her when she wanted to slip away from the house on occasion and she would help me get to stay in town a while longer by calling Granny and telling her I was helping in the beauty shop where she worked.

Margie went to work at the beauty shop when she was about seventeen years old. When she had to work late, I would walk up to town and sweep the beauty shop floor for fifty cents and then I would walk her home.

If you have read any of my other stories, you probably remember how dark it got from three ditch bridge to our house which was about the longest quarter mile in the world, especially if you were scared of the dark to begin with, which "she" was.

One night there was about ten to fifteen people at our house for supper when Margie called and said she was about finished at the beauty shop and would I meet her at the three ditch bridge and walk the rest of the way home with her. Being the loving little "brother" I was; I told her sure, that I would be there in twenty minutes.

One of my cousin's (Carmelita) had just married and she and her husband (Bill Smith) were visiting. I told Bill that I sure knew a way to have some real fun with Margie. After he heard my plan, he agreed. It went something like this; I would meet Margie at the bridge while Bill hid in the road ditch about half way between the bridge and our house, he would wait until we passed him and jump from the ditch and scare the hebegeebees out of her. Man that was going to be more fun that you could imagine.

I walked to the bridge and it was pitch black that night. Darker than usual with overcast skies and it was just a glooming night. Perfect for what we were about to do. She wasn't there when I got there, guess I was early just waiting for the fun to begin. I sat upon the railing of the three ditch bridge in the darkness that was soon closing in on me. Soon, I hear her coming and began to get exited again. As soon as she got to me, she grabbed my hand and said, let's get on home, that it was too spooky out that night. Crap, now she's starting to scare me. Being the man I was at fourteen, I told her to take it easy, I wouldn't let anything happen to her, hehe.

Because it was so dark that night and of course, there was no traffic to see the road from their headlights, we walked as close to the middle of the road as we could. As we came close to where Bill was hiding on the left side of the road, I tried to ease us over toward him to make this even better. We walked another fifty feet and, no Bill. I thought he had gotten tired waiting on us and went on back to the house, so I moved back to the middle of the road, when it happened! Bill had taken it upon himself to add a little flavor to this adventure and had hidden on the other side of the road and also, brought along his 12 gauge shotgun for a little added sound effects. All I remember when the shotgun went off and what sounded like a heard of buffalo coming out of the road ditch was me running at full speed, Aunt Margie flailing behind me like a rag doll I couldn't shake loose. When we hit the old railroad tie across the road ditch which we used as a walkway to our yard, I am positive Margie never touched the ground until I dropped her on the living room floor on the way to my bedroom to change clothes, not because I had peed all over mine, but we always dressed for supper in my part of the country!

CHRISTMAS VACATION 1969

By: Jim Ferguson

The year was 1969. The time was Christmas vacation. For the first time in my life we were going on a family vacation--other than going to Granny's and Grandpaw's house. We were going to California. I had an aunt and uncle who lived in Winter Haven, California which is across the state line of Yuma, Arizona. My dad also had a brother who lived in Los Angles and we were going to visit them also. A big trip for a country boy! Dad had bought a new truck that fall, put a camper shell on the back, and built bench seats across the front and down each side for us all to sit on. Mom had put blankets in the camper for us to keep warm. There were nine of us who went and we were packed in like a bunch of gypsies. There was Dad, Mom, Grandmother (who was close to seventy years old and she rode in the back of the truck the whole way), three sisters, one brother, one cousin and, of course, ME. In addition there were enough clothes for every one for one week as well as food for snacks and lunches. First class all the way. Really, the trip was an adventure and we had a wonderful time. We spent the first night in eastern Texas where we even got a motel room and had dinner at a diner. I had one of the best burgers and fries I have ever eaten in my life. The burger was huge and there more fries than I could eat and, believe me when I was seventeen years old, I could eat. After we had eaten that night and while the others were bathing, my cousin, Bill Cooper, and I decided we needed to take a look around the town a little bit. We soon found ourselves in a pool hall/bar. Now a pool hall was something I was used to as I had been playing pool all my life but a bar--that was a new experience. After having played only one game of pool we were asked to leave after Bill tried to buy himself a beer without proper ID. This night should have been an omen of things to come. Rising early the next morning we packed up and continued our trip. It took most of the day to get to El Paso and then out of Texas so we spent that night in New Mexico putting this country boy a long way from home completely out of his element. After the family ate dinner and found a room, Bill and I once again took a walk about and once again located a pool hall. Since we were not asked to leave this time, we were able to play a few games before heading back to the motel and, yes, Bill managed to buy himself a beer this time. We all rose early the next morning and drove for a few hours before we stopped at Carlsbad Caverns in New Mexico. After touring the Caverns for a few hours (which is a really big cave--one of the world's largest) we resumed traveling and reached my aunt's home late that afternoon. For the next few days we enjoyed the company of relatives and enjoyed quite a bit of fresh fruit from the trees growing on my aunt's property--lemons that were as big as grapefruits and oranges that were…well, they were huge! We did a lot of sightseeing. We went to the Yuma Territorial Prison which was used back in the 1800s as a jail for the outlaws and bandits. It was such a very harsh place that few made it out alive. We went to the sand dunes that covered several miles of desert near Winter Haven--nothing but big piles of sand that looked like something you would see in movies (in fact a lot of movies were filmed there) where the characters rode the camels across from oasis to oasis. It was an amazing sight and was perfect for riding dune buggies. One of the days we were there my cousin Bill and I slipped off and went to Algodones, a small Mexican village just southwest of Winter Haven. The stores and shops were made of adobe and had dirt floors--a true Mexican village. It was also a place where we had no business being but we made it in and out without any trouble. Since my aunt worked for the Fort Yuma Quechan Indian Reservation she was able to get permission for us to attend a dance on the reservation one night. Now I had never been around any Indians before much less seen so many pretty Indian woman. I fell in love several times that night and would have loved to have been able to spend several weeks in Winter Haven after that night to pursue a couple of the

Indian princesses. But it wasn't to be. We only had one more night left in Winter Haven before moving on to Los Angeles. The last night is when the trouble began. The next evening Bill and I went to Yuma to the Golden Cue. While we were playing pool we met a couple of airmen who were stationed at the air force base just outside of town. During the course of the evening we decided we would go to San Luis, a town south of the border--into Mexico. It was a town where many of the military men would go to have a few beers, dance with the Mexican women, and fall in love by the hour. This was most definitely a place a couple of young boys from the boot heel of Missouri should not be going. Now I'm not telling you this story to be bragging about anything that went on that night. No, it's just the opposite. I'm telling it to you so you can see and realize how easy it is for kids (such as I was at that time) to get themselves into trouble--not to mention the fact that we were in another country where we couldn't just pick up the phone and call Dad to come and get us. However at that age you think you are ten feet tall and bullet proof and you do not realize just how dumb and naive you really are. Upon reaching the border we hired a taxi to take us outside of town a couple miles to where the clubs were located. The agreed-upon price for the ride was a dollar a piece since there were five of us in the group. Five dollars was a fair price I thought. However upon arriving at the clubs, the driver informed us it would be five dollars each and that is when the trouble began. Feeling as though the taxi driver was trying to take advantage of us, we refused to pay and began arguing with him. Five dollars was a lot of money and I only had ten dollars on me and I had no desire to give it to him. Luckily, before "push came to shove" a Mexican policeman approached and explained to us the rules of Mexico. We could pay the taxi driver or we could go to jail. This may have been my first trip as a world traveler but I knew I wanted no part of a Mexican jail causing me to change my mind and decide that five dollars was probably a very fair price after all. After taking in the sights that night we walked the two or three miles across the Mexican desert back to the border. Awaking early the next morning our family loaded up into the truck and headed for Los Angeles with my Aunt Barbara and Uncle Alex Lee and their two boys following. While we were in L.A. we went to Disneyland where we all had a great time. However I do wonder sometimes about my mother's wisdom. She decided since bill and I were older we should be the ones who were in charge of keeping up with my youngest sister, Karma. That did turn out to be an advantage for us as far as riding all the rides. Since the lines to get on the rides were so long we devised a wonderful plan. (I always believe in having a plan.) What we would do is send Karma to the front of the line or close to it. Our logic was that she since was only seven or eight years old, the people wouldn't fuss at her for breaking line. Once she was settled into position, Bill and I would start calling her name as though she were lost until we reached her. Then of course we would just stay with her near the front of the line. We repeated this procedure on every ride throughout the rest of the day. By the days end we had ridden all the rides Disneyland had to offer. On one of the other nights we were in L.A., my cousins and I went to Hollywood and Vine where we saw the movie stars and the famous foot prints, dropped by the Play Boy Club to see the play boy bunnies. Of course we were not permitted to go inside it. We didn't really think we would be admitted but, hey, you never know. We also visited the ocean while we were in L.A. and were just amazed. I had no earthly idea then that within a year and a half I would be sailing on that very same ocean on an American aircraft carrier. But as always time changes all things. Our trip came to a close way too soon but it was a vacation I have never forgotten. We all thoroughly enjoyed the trip. It gave me the desire to travel and I have travelled quite a bit since that time. While in the service I was stationed at Imperial Beach, California just south of San Diego. While there I traveled as much of California as I could and went to the beaches, the mountains, and the deserts. Although it is a beautiful state and a nice place to visit, I wouldn't want to live there--too many people for this country boy.

Great memories.

CLEAT MONSTERS

By: Terry Weldon

I grew up living a half mile out of town of Gideon, Missouri, which generally never bothered me. Even when I was very young I would walk to school and back and never thought a thing about it. On the way to school, there were four or five school buses that passed my house every morning. I could have stepped out on the porch and any one of them would have stopped and picked me up. Most mornings I would go ahead and walk, or if I did ride the bus, it was generally Vernon Tolbert's bus. In the afternoon there was always someone walking from the school to the ballpark across the road from my house that I could walk with.

Also, living in a small town like Gideon, it was pretty hard to walk anywhere because you knew everyone and everyone knew you, so as soon as you hit the road, someone stopped to pick you up. I remember hitch-hiking from Gideon, all the way to Malden, (10 miles) to sell Grit newspapers, visit cousins, or see a movie without fear of being abducted, or molested. Unfortunately, that is no longer the case. You can't even let your kids play in the yard these days. It is a shame, that today's children are missing a fantastic part of their lives, but it isn't their fault.

When I got old enough and started playing baseball and the game wasn't being played across the road from our house, I simply got ready and walked across the road. After the game I generally would walk with several people on their way back into town and stop off at our house. Because the coach would sometimes drag the field after the game, I would be at home and in bed before the ballpark lights were turned out.

If the games were "away" games, I would walk to school and catch the bus with everyone else going to the game. I would get involved with my friends on the way back home and remain on the bus as it passed my home and ride on into town, causing me to have to walk back home.

Gideon was a small town, but it did have street lights until you reached three ditch bridge heading East from Gideon, as you crossed the bridge the street lights were non-existent. From that bridge it was a little over a quarter-mile to our house and it was darker than dark! If it was a full moon I could see just fine, however, when there was no moon, the only way I knew I was heading down the road correctly was when an on-coming car's headlights shined on the white lines for ten seconds.

Now for some reason, to the best of my knowledge, there never was a moon out when we had an away game. Which means when I had to walk over three ditch bridge into the darkness, I could hear them, the cleat monsters! I could never see them, but I knew they were right there on my heels, breathing down the back of my neck. They were extremely fast, a car could come by and I would stop quickly, turn to look, and they were not there. After the car had passed and I began walking again, there were right there again. I would speed up to a trot and so would they, if I weaved across the road left to right, so did they. The strangest things about the cleat monsters was when I crossed the railroad tie bridge we had across the road ditch in front of the house, they were gone. They must have been afraid of our house or something, because I never heard them in our yard.

CORN COBS AND MUD BALLS

By: Jim Ferguson

Back in the day, one of the things country boys and, sometimes country girls, did for entertainment was to have a good ole corn cob fight. I have often wondered if this isn't where dodge ball originated. Now to have a really good corn cob fight there should be at least three people. It can be done with fewer kids, but more is better. If there are only two people playing, it is easier to anticipate which direction the next flying corn cob is coming. If there are more kids, the element of surprise is there as to where it came from or who hit you. Now all you need is, of course, a good supply of corn cobs and a place to hide with the preferred place being in a barn loft with bales of straw or hay. (You can use the bales to build your defenses--a wall is good so the opposing forces couldn't be for sure where you would pop up next to send the corn cob their way.) Now the selection of the corn cobs is a big issue. The best ones are a little on the "wet" side because the heavier they are improves your accuracy. Now if you can find one that has lain up on the old feed lot and has maybe soaked up a little, well, let's say "cow patty" that is good. Nothing takes the fight out of someone quicker than getting hit up beside the head with a cow-patty-soaked corn cob. Now one of the best corn cob fights I ever had the privilege to be in took place at Chris Elam's place. His dad Roy trained quarter horses for a living and that included breaking the young ones. You know there are some stories to be told about that also. It seemed that Roy Elam loved nothing better than putting Chris and me on the young, unbroken horses for no other reason than to see how long it would take to get our butts thrown off the horses. One other thing I'd like to mention about Roy Elam. He served in the U.S. Navy during World War II and was on the USS Missouri when the peace treaty was signed with Japan. In some photos of the signing Roy can be seen in the background. Back to mud balls...Chris had a barn that was perfect for corncob fights: high loft, hay, and plenty of wet corn cobs. On this particular Sunday afternoon Chris, Jimmy Bostic, and I gathered up a good supply of corn cobs, moved our hay bales into position, and commenced firing at one another for the better part of the afternoon with no serious injuries with the exception of one bloody nose which I am proud to say was delivered by me. I caught Jimmy right in the ole kisser. Smack! However the day wasn't quite over and right before quitting time he repaid me with a good solid hit right on the cheek. To this day I still believe that corn cob had some corn left on it because it took the first two or three layers of hide right off.

During those periods of time that we couldn't get any good corn cobs, our back up ammunition was mud balls. The best thing to do was make your mud balls a day or two in advance to allow for proper drying time. Good gumbo worked the best. To make them, grab yourself a hand full of mud, roll it into a ball about the size of a golf ball, and let it dry a day or so. You wanted at least a good crust on it but preferably you wanted it bone dry. We also discovered that by putting the mud balls on a stick, we could throw it two or three times further. It can also be done with a green persimmon—great ammunition. Looking back on those days, I think it's a wonder we weren't hurt worse than we were but we always seemed to heal. It's a shame kids today can't do this. Why just think of all the things they would have to do just to have a good corn cob fight. They would have to don helmets, eye protection, and throat guards at the very least along with producing legal papers saying their parents would not sue if poor Johnny was hurt. Add to the list umpires, penalty boxes for the times you hit someone who had their back turned, and EMTs with ambulances on the ready. Might also need to add skilled defense lawyers for Moms and Dads just in case the judicial system decided they were negligent parents. I'm afraid we have taken the fun away from the kids along with some good memories.

Thanks for the memories.

DEER CAMP

By: Jim Ferguson

The saying, "What happens in Vegas stays in Vegas" should also apply to deer camp...but, what would be the fun in that?

I started deer hunting with a very good friend of mine, Ron Yarbro, too many years ago to count. I first got to know Ron and his family when he came to Gideon in the eighties as principal of the school. We became great friends and hunted and fished together. After they left Gideon and moved to Ellington, Missouri, we would visit back and forth as families often do. And that is when the deer camps began. That allowed us the chance to maintain a friendship that would last for years and year and also granted us the wonderful opportunity to watch our sons grow into young men. We have collected many memories of our boys! There was the case of the famous words shouted by one of the boys after we heard the firing of a rifle, "HEY, DAD, I KILLED A DEER!" We immediately heard more firing and the words, "HEY, DAD, I KILLED ANOTHER ONE!!" Or the day one of the other boys killed two nice bucks with in an hour. I remember the time that my oldest son, Lyle, killed one of the biggest bucks that was killed in the course of the camps. He killed it the last day of the season with just a few minutes of sun light left. After he shot the deer it ended up at the bottom of a steep hill. Oh, the fun we had trying to get it loaded onto a three wheeler and back up the hill in the dark while fighting the brush and trees. After getting it to the top where we could load it into the truck, Ron told Lyle, "The next time, wait until the deer is closer to the top before you shoot." There is also the time that Lyle got lost and spent the night in a snow storm before making it back to camp the next morning.

One year when we were camped west of Ellington near Current River, it came such a flood that we could not get back to town for two days. Yes, we were stranded on top of the hill and everything was wet. A miserable weekend but a great memory.

Then there are the stories of the three wheeler and me. One was when I had been hunting at the bottom of the hill we called Billy Goat Hill. Upon returning to the three wheeler to head back to camp, I discovered the three wheeler wouldn't start. While I was there trying to start it and, mind you, doing a lot of fussing, Chris, Ron's son, came by in his ole jeep offering to give me a tow back to camp. Eagerly, we tied a rope to the jeep and three wheeler and up the hill we went. Now everything went fine as long as we were going up the hill but as we approached the camp there was a downgrade. After years of experience of raising boys as well as some of my own misguided adventures, I should have known better than to do what we were doing. As we started down this hill, the three wheeler started picking up speed.

I forgot to mention previously that not only would it not start--it would not stop because the breaks had been worn out for years. The boys knew how to ride it in this condition; however, the problem was I DIDN'T know how to handle it. Now the faster I went, the faster Chris went because he was trying to stay in front of me. At some point, I reached the speed where I passed him. But that isn't the real problem. If you have enough rope, the problem comes when you run out of rope. Now when I reached that point, the three wheeler stopped but I didn't. I went over the handle bars, out through the woods, and ended up against a tree, which is a good thing considering I could have ended up under the jeep. And since there were no bones broken, all was well and it did provide some good entertainment for every one who was sitting around the camp fire with a front row seat to see my performance.

Now there are other stories of the same three wheeler. For instance I was trying to catch Ron to give him his hat that had blown off of his four wheeler. Hearing me approach he stopped but, once again, I didn't. Yep I slammed into the back of his four wheeler and off I went rolling across the road up against another tree. Or the time Chris and I were both on his four wheeler going up a steep hill and it flipped back over on us. Looking back I think I would have been much better off walking. Time has passed. Ron and I have aged and enjoy more comfortable deer seasons. Chris and Adam and Micheal have grown up and have families of their own. We lost Lyle in 1998 which was a loss to both families. Ron and I have maintained our friendship and continue to hunt and fish together.

I tip my hat to you Big Guy and thank you for the memories.

EDUCATION AND LIFE'S LESSONS

By: Jim Ferguson

As a young lad I started my education process by attending Gideon Elementary School. I remember waiting at the end of the driveway leading to our house for the bus to come and pick up my sisters and me for the long ride to school. Mr. Carlee Moore was our bus driver. From day number one I remember how he was always looking into the big mirror keeping an eye on the older boys who gathered in the back of the bus. Carlee ran a tight ship as best he could but even then there were always paper wads being thrown forward and rubber bands being shot at the girls and younger kids sitting toward the front of the bus. There were times he would stop, come to the rear of the bus, and escort one of the older boys to a seat up front. On some occasions he would put them off the bus and make them walk the rest of the way home. I still visit with a couple of those boys: Larry and Randall Bentley. I guess the discipline and long walks home worked for they both became pillars of their communities. Upon arriving at school my first thought was that this was going to be great since there were swings, monkey bars to climb on, slides, merry go rounds, and a lot of kids to play with. Oh, little did I know that there were strings attached to the playground. One thing was you didn't get to play all day. There was this issue of sitting inside a class room listening to a teacher who was expecting you to learn to read, write, spell, and do arithmetic. Unfortunately my theory was why should I learn to read when I could be outside playing? I knew no one to whom I could write a letter; therefore, if I wasn't going to be writing why would I need to learn to spell? As for arithmetic I hadn't any money so why did I need to learn to count? However with the assistance of Mr. Shelton (the grade school principle), the teachers were able to remold my ideas of school so the education process continued. But I continued to sit for hours looking out the classroom windows day dreaming of things I could be doing outside. Being luckier than some who had the same attitude I had, it only took twelve years for me to complete school. As far as being educated--I'm not. My school career was a total flop. Looking back I do wish I had spent more time studying than looking out those windows. I did learn to count which has served me well because now when I buy something I know the exact change I should be getting back with out the use of a calculator or computer. I also learned to read and that is something I fell in love with a few years later. My first serious attempts at reading complete books were those written by the author Louis L'Amour, a greater writer and story teller. With him as my guide I have marched across Europe in *The Walking Drum*; I've sailed the oceans and fought pirates in *Fair Blows the Wind*; I've settled new lands and fought Indians in the *Far Blue Mountains* alongside Barnabas Sackett. I've traveled up the Mississippi River on a raft with Echo, the great granddaughter of Barnabas. I've explored the vast west with Jubal Sackett, a son of Barnabas. I was with him the day he rode a white buffalo. I've ridden alongside the Sackett brothers, Tell, Tyrel, and Orrin, as they trailed cattle and fought and tamed the mining towns of the west. I've learned with a well-written book, the author not only tells you the story but also takes you on an adventure. If the author doesn't make you feel as though you are living the story along with him, then he hasn't done his job. Throughout the course of the last thirty years I have read hundreds of books including murder mysteries, adventures, and novels, science fiction (my least favorite) and have enjoyed the stories of many great writers. Now I do not consider myself a writer. No, I'm just a country boy who worked hard and played hard when not working and tried to enjoy life. I have, however, enjoyed telling you my stories. I do wish I had studied more in school so the trips I have tried to take you on would have been more enjoyable for you. And as always, time passes and changes all things. Now that the hot days of summer are just about gone and the cool days of fall are upon us and I sit here looking out the window, I'm once again daydreaming of more adventures in life. I truly hope you have enjoyed the stories I've shared with you. Later, I will be back hopefully with new adventures. Until then grab a good book and take a trip.

Thanks to all the authors for the memories and to you my friends.

FREE GO CART

By: Terry Weldon

One of the weekends I was spending at Uncle Edd's comes back to me often. Around nine o'clock one Saturday morning Dan and I were stirring around in the back yard looking for something to tinker with, we were going through the junk pile, which was more like a vein of gold to a couple of 12 year old boys when we ran upon a Briggs and Stratton engine. We both spotted this gem at the same time, turned and looked each other in the eyes with the exact same thought running through our head; we are positive we could have us a go cart running by supper. It was going to be a classic two seater. I would handle the steering wheel and Dan would man the hand brake and we didn't need no stinking roll bars!

Before this masterpiece could come to life, we had to get the Briggs running. Because we were already master mechanics at twelve years old, that shouldn't be a problem. We took the engine out of the junk pile and hurried to the "pit" to get it going. The pit at that time was a fifty-five gallon barrel with a couple of two by fours laid across it. It was the ideal work bench, we could reach everything on top of the engine and the crankshaft hung down into the barrel out of the way. Perfectly stable.

Of course there was no cover on the engine and the flywheel was open to the elements on top. With no cover on it, that meant there was no starter rope, just a groove where the rope went. This was not a problem for us, we simply found us a three foot section of clothesline and we were off to the races, so to speak. I wrapped the clothesline cord around the groove on top of the engine a couple of times while my pit crew, (Dan), held fast to the engine block. I gave it a good firm jerk on the cord and we both almost pissed our pants, the cotton picking thing started! As we were dancing around like a couple of school girls, we noticed the engine was vibrating around the top of the two by fours and was about to slip off and down into the barrel. I ran over to the barrel as the engine was slipping off the board and heading down. I couldn't let that happen, so I reached down into the barrel and grabbed the top of the engine by the flywheel... did I mention the engine was running and there was no cover on it! Yes, I actually did grab that engine by the "spinning" flywheel. Needless to say, I let go faster than I grabbed it.

We both stood there a second wondering what had happened and what to do next when Dan said "is that blood on your hand"? Looking down at the thumb on my left hand, I won't lie to you, I nearly fainted. The left half of the nail was curled back from the cuticle to the tip of the thumb and I could clearly see my heartbeat!

Being the cool guy that I am, I looked at Dan and said, "does that look right to you"? Because it was numb, we could sort of chuckle about it until the blood flow became more of a spurt than a drip.

All of the women were gone somewhere and Uncle Edd was asleep after working midnight shift. We walked into his bedroom, dreading to have to wake him up, but knowing this was not good, Dan nudged him and as he was trying to wake and come to his senses, I stuck, what now was looking more like a young squash than a thumb right up in his face, blood pouring everywhere. He jumped like it was the mafia tossing a horse head in bed with him. Being cool like I was, I said, "should we do something about this"? Then to be honest, the rest of that day is a blur…

FALL IN THE FIFTIES

By: Jim Ferguson

The era is the fifties and the time is late summer or early fall. After working all summer long, we've got all the cotton chopped and the vegetables from the garden are all canned and put up for the coming winter: green beans, peas, squash, corn, okra, and tomatoes. The cabbage has been turned into kraut, cucumbers have been turned into pickles, and peaches from Campbell (two bushels) have been peeled, cut up, and canned.

Work in the fields has slowed other than some weeding of the soybeans. The corn is ready for harvest. Since Dad doesn't have a corn header or combine, it will be harvested by a local farmer who owns such equipment. This arrangement allows us more time to get ready for the next big push which will be cotton. We spend our days now planning for it. The cotton trailers must be mended by putting in new floor boards, wire mended on the sides, all bearings must be checked and greased, tires checked and replaced because having a flat on a loaded cotton trailer is something you really want to prevent! Other preparations for the upcoming cotton picking season have also been made. For us, it included sending letters to the families in Arkansas who made the trip each year to help with the harvest. One of the families is the Lawrences' who lived in Big Flat, Arkansas. They would arrive each year with everything they needed for the next month or two stacked in and tied to their pickup truck. They would move into a small house on our farm that was only used for that purpose. Since it sat empty the rest of the year, it made a great playing place for us kids on rainy days. As the days approached and the cotton fields began to resemble a white sheet spread across the fields, more and more families moved into other farmhouses owned by other farmers in southeast Missouri. One of these was O. B. Sisk. He was a friend of Dad's and spent several Sunday mornings at our home drinking coffee and playing checkers with Dad.

Schools were let out for what was called "cotton picking vacation." By no means was it a vacation! We would rise early each morning to begin picking. Kids of all ages would pick right along with the adults. The pick sacks would range from tote sacks to burlap bags to nine foot sacks. We would pick and pack and pick some more until our sacks were full. Then we would throw it over our shoulders and carry it to the trailer where it was weighed. The amount was written down in a book to keep up with how much each person was paid at the end of the day. This is what drew people from all over to southeast Missouri in the fall. We were paid three dollars per hundred pounds. Now if you were a family of five or six and averaged 250 to 300 pounds a day per person that was a lot of money. I have known a few people who could pick as many as 400 or 500 pounds of cotton a day, but that was far more than I ever reached. However we stopped picking by hand by the time I was eleven or twelve years of age. My all-time high was a little over 200 pounds. Although the work was hard there were good times to be enjoyed. For example, in the field there was always someone who would be singing or telling jokes or old stories. An occasional cotton bowl thrown by an older kid would sail nearby or even hit you, or some kid would be scolded for loafing or sometimes the mom or dad would pull up a cotton stalk and give the kid a good thrashing for lying on their sack. Lunches were eaten under the cotton trailers for the purpose of taking advantage of the shade. Bologna was often the main fare. Sometimes sodas would be available but, if not, we would drink water. Now for those of you who have never eaten in the field with the wind blowing dust all over your food, you sure have missed it.

As the days grew shorter and fall chilled the air, we all knew brighter days were ahead because the carnival always came to town during the fall. For us kids it meant we could take a dollar and ride all the rides; eat cotton candy and corn dogs; and get sick. Also during the fall, the apple peddler would make his rounds throughout the countryside selling apples--which were a treat. Mom and Dad would always buy a bushel of apples and set them in a back room of the house (which was always cooler). There is nothing like the aroma of apples to spice up the house unless it would be the aroma of a freshly-baked apple pie.

And as always, time passes and changes all things. The days of picking cotton by hand are long gone as are the days of riding in the cotton trailer while it is being pulled to the gin in town. Gone also are the days of sitting around the kitchen table helping Mom place an order for new clothes through the Sears Roebuck catalog or waiting to open them when the postman delivered the package to your door. I don't miss the days of picking cotton, but I do miss the memories of families working together in what seemed a simpler time.

Great memories.

FIREFLIES, WHIPPOORWILLS, AND OTHER NIGHT THINGS

By: Jim Ferguson

It's dark. I wish they would leave a night light on for me. I know the boogieman is under the bed — well, if not there he is in the closet. I don't understand why Mom and Dad made me go outside earlier tonight and put the dogs in their pen. They knew it was dark and they knew something could have gotten me. I have heard them several times in the past talking about being goblins outside. Oh yeah, Dad called me a scaredy cat. Well if what they say about goblins is true then it doesn't mean I was scared; rather it means I have good sense. It is a shame that this is how some children were brought up: being taught to fear the night. The fact is the night is a great time to be outside. There are things to see and hear that you cannot see or hear at any other time. Take fireflies (lightning bugs). Do you ever see them during the day? I remember as a young kid we looked forward to the time of the year when the fireflies would make their appearance. We would all run around the yard trying to catch them and put some of them in a fruit jar. Or we would squeeze the tail off on our fingers declaring they were diamond rings or on the earlobes of girls saying they were wearing diamond earrings. I have done this for as long as I can remember and still do so today. This last spring I had the joy of teaching my granddaughter how to make diamond rings out of them.

Another joy of life that is exclusive to the night is the song of a whippoorwill. Whippoorwills are nocturnal birds that start their mating call in the spring as the sun sets and they continue through the night. I have enjoyed the evening call for years. Their call sounds like their name: "WHIP POOR WILL" and is often repeated many, many times before they stop to rest. A few years ago my wife Brenda and I witnessed one at our cabin sing his love song for thirty-six times before taking a break. After a few seconds, he began again. Now I will say if you are camping or trying to sleep they can be annoying after a few minutes.

There were always things to do when we were young at night especially when we would have company. While Mom and Dad were inside talking to their friends, we kids would be out playing hide and seek. No flash lights were needed because we just used the stars and moonlight. We could and would play for hours. Now I am sure a lot of you remember how to play the game but for those that don't it is really simple. There is a home base and one person must close their eyes and count to a designated number. While he or she was doing this, the others would find a place to hide. When the person finished counting, he or she would begin their search for the others. If you were hidden and thought you could run to home base without being tagged, you could attempt it. However if you were tagged then you became the hunter and the game continued.

Now for us boys there were other things to do at night. For instance if we had an outdoor light, we could always bet there would be toad frogs sitting close by trying to eat the bugs that were drawn to the light. As you know frogs and boys go together like well...just like frogs and boys! They just fit. As young boys, my friends and I often caught frogs and had jumping contests with them. We also loved chasing the girls with them because the screams of girls were priceless at that time of our lives. Now frogs have this unique thing about them. Because their tongues are very sticky, anything it touches goes to the mouth and it is hard for them to spit it back out. Now this is a good thing to know since you can have a lot of fun when you have this information about them. The theory was (as I was taught) that you could load a frog up so full with bee-bees that he could not hop. However I was never able to do this although I have fed them a lot of bee-bees. We would just what roll the bee-bees in front of the frog. It would assume it was an insect and out his tongue would come--very accurately. Once the bee-bee was on the sticky tongue, into his mouth it would go. I must say that watching them try to spit it out was funny. More often than not he would swallow it. I have fed them as many as twenty bee-bees before they would stop grabbing them.

Another fun night activity was taking our northern cousins snipe hunting. Now I'll not tell you the details of this adventure, but if you would like to go sometime let me know. It would be an honor to take you on one of America's favorite hunts. So as you can see the nights should not be a scary thing for children. Instead we should teach them the fun they can have.--more fun than the games they play now with these contraptions we buy for them at Wal-Mart. The benefit of this is that you spend more time with your children and thereby create more lasting memories. One night just take them away from the city lights so they can really grasp the beauty of the stars and the moon. But as always, time changes all things. This is true about the night sky, too. The stars and moon have been shining since time began but we know there are satellites in space now. On a clear night you can see them orbiting the earth. Go out and look for them; they are there. And yes it is true--it can be dark. While I was serving in the U.S. Navy aboard the *USS Cleveland*, we were at sea doing war exercises. As the scenario went we were declared dead in the water which meant no lights aboard ship. The cloud cover cooperated by hiding the light of the moon and stars. It was really dark. As I stepped onto the cat walk I realized that I couldn't even count the fingers on my own hands. The darkness was astounding! It made me feel totally alone and caused me to consider the men who have been lost overboard or who have gone down on sinking ships in total darkness. The loneliness and fright they experienced knowing the chance of being found was slim had to be awful. So unless you are in those conditions, enjoy the amazing night life our Father has provided for us.

Thanks for the (dark) memories.

HELP A BROTHER OUT

By: Terry Weldon

My mother, Joe BEASLEY Weldon had multiple sclerosis and passed away at the age of twenty nine in 1954. She was in a wheelchair for the last few years of her life. I was four years old when she passed and I don't remember much about her. I remember that she had a big collie dog that stayed underneath her wheelchair. I often wondered how it kept from getting it's tail ran over, but it didn't. I also remember that mom had a hair brush that she kept tucked away by her leg. When me or my brother, Jack (Puncho) or my sister, Patricia (Sissie) did something we shouldn't have done, she would call us to come to her for our punishment. We had a great deal of respect for our mom, or we weren't too bright and didn't hesitate to go right over to her take our punishment from the back of that brush on our little behinds. She would probably get in trouble today for using the hairbrush on us. Some sort of child abuse. I personally think we need a lot more hair brushes being used in this country now days.

Mom would make all of our clothes using my Granny Beasley's treadle sewing machine. Because her legs had drawn up in the chair from the multiple sclerosis, she would turn the sewing machine with her hand on top. Sometimes one of us children would lie underneath her and peddle for her. I still don't know how she managed it.

I think it was the mailman, who was either a journalist for our local paper, or just loved to gossip passed the word around town about mom and how she was a single mom, making her children's clothes trying to survive. Some of the town's people got together and bought mom a new electric sewing. She was as proud as a peacock and although I don't remember, I suspect we kids had lots of new clothes for a while.

While the rest of the family worked in the cotton fields every year, mom would cook and care for the house when she was able. Me, my brother and sister were too young to be in the fields working, so we were home with mom. I was too little to do much, but my brother Puncho was just the right age to do everything from, climbing into the cabinets and retrieving pots, pans, and bowels to going out into the garden for vegetables.

One day, Puncho, who was around eight years old was really busy doing tasks for mom and I felt a little sorry for him. Mom told him to take the trash can out of the kitchen, dump it into the burning barrel and burn it. He whimpered a little about how much he was having to do, Sissie was a girl and they didn't do trash back then, and I was too small do it and mom wouldn't tell me too. He was complaining and saying that it just wasn't fair. Mom was off in the bedroom sewing and Sissie was out on the front porch playing with a doll or something, so I decided

I would give him a hand. I was around four years old and couldn't pick the trash can up to take it out side and burn the trash, so I set the trash can on fire in the kitchen! Made perfect sense when I was four…

FISHING WITH CLEO

By: Jim Ferguson

After having written several stories on my fishing and hunting experiences I was asked by some why I hadn't written one on the times I fished with Cleo Pattillo. The reason I haven't is that I just don't know where to begin. Until I started fishing with Cleo, all of my fishing experiences took place on the ditches in southeast Missouri while fishing for catfish, perch, and carp with one exception. My first time crappie fishing I went with Jim Johnson and we fished one of the chutes of the Mississippi River. After we ate fried crappie, supplied by Cleo, one night at my in-law's, it was suggested to me by my wife at the time to give Cleo a call to see if I could go fishing with him sometime. A suggestion she probably wished she had never made but one I'm glad to this day she thought of it. Even though I have spent thousands upon thousands of dollars and many days doing it, I'm still in love with it. After I made the call to Cleo he told me he was going the next day and I was welcome to come along. Now Cleo was a fisherman's fisherman, he was old school. In the early days of fishing with him, we used minnows. He knew every stump and brush pile in Wappapella Lake that held fish. (Not all stumps and brush piles do.) This was in the days before depth finders and took years of fishing to find those stumps and brush piles. He freely shared that knowledge with me and with others. He was forever laughing at me every time I'd get hung up in a brush pile or lose a fish before I could get it into the boat. But he would also tell me, "Jim, I think you have the touch to make a good fisherman." As Cleo has done, I've fished with a lot of different people during the last forty years and have found it to be true some will make good fisherman and some, for reasons I don't know, will never get the hang of it. Randy Jackson probably caught on faster than anyone I ever started out fishing. He also became a big lover of the sport. Cleo and I fished a lot of years together. I always liked listening to his stories and his songs and laughing at his forever dripping nose in the winter. We fished every waterhole in southeast Missouri as well as venturing off to other states such as Mississippi, Tennessee, and Arkansas. Some of my favorite memories of fishing with him came when Cleo, Toby Jordon, Rayburn Bell, Carl Chamberlin, and I went to Millwood Lake located between Hope and Texarkana, Arkansas. (There is another story about one of those trips to Millwood Lake when I went with Ray Halterman. We met Bill Clinton between his governorships and, after meeting him, I'd say all the stories of him being a womanizer would be true.) Cleo and I made this trip to Millwood Lake for several years always staying at the Rail Car Inn. The owner had taken box cars and turned them in to cabins. We always had a blast together and always caught a lot of fish. A few weeks before we were to leave on the last trip we made to Millwood, Cleo had a heart attack. I went to see him in the hospital and mentioned that I hated that he wouldn't get to go with us that year. He quite quickly informed me that he would be ready to go and he did go. While we were packing to leave on our trip, I told him if he had a heart attack while we were there, I wasn't going to bring him home but I would put him on a bus and ship him home. He told me to just prop him up in the boat, put a pole in his hand, and he'd bet he could still out fish us.

As with all my stories, time passes and changes all things. Cleo is no longer with us, but the memories of the days I spent in a boat with him are still fresh and enjoyable to remember but not only for me. I wasn't the only one Cleo mentored because he was the mentor to a lot of young men from Gideon who wanted to learn the art of fishing. It would be safe to say we all thank you for the memories. I tip my hat to you, Sir.

HIS EYES SHINED

By: Terry Weldon

I have a friend from my hometown, Gideon, Missouri who began to put his memories in short stories. I enjoyed reading those stories, because I could relate to them so, I thought I could try my hand at it.

When my wife and I, along with our three children were in the USAF, stationed at Nellis AFB, NV, between 1977 and 1983 we wanted to do everything we could to teach our three children, some might say, to the point of being obsessed, right and wrong. I was a disciplinarian, which is effective, but may not be the best child rearing method.

I was a Scoutmaster, Weblos leader, couched Tee ball and soccer all at the same time for several years trying to involve our children in good, clean, wholesome activities.

One summer we were having an "Arrow of Light" ceremony out in the Valley of Fire state park. We spent hours setting up campsites, preparing the props to be used for the ceremony and trying to remember our lines for the presentation. There were five boys who had worked very hard to earn the highest award you can receive in the Cub Scouts. One of the boys to receive the award that night was my son, Jeff Weldon. I had pushed him hard to get to this point in his Scouting career and I remember thinking about how to present these awards without showing more pride for Jeff's achievement than the other boys.

The sun was setting and we gathered all of the Scouts and their families around what was soon to be our campfire set against a thirty foot flat rock wall that will reflect the campfire perfectly. We brought out the American flag, said our pledge, and was ready to start the campfire. The setting sun shined over to the top of the next thirty foot tall rock where an Indian warrior came up from the back of the rock, raised his bow, released a flaming arrow, (on a wire) which landed right in the center of the "friendship fire". The fire was roaring to life in seconds. Perfect in every way. Everyone there was awe-struck. Looking back to the top of the rock and the Indian had vanished into the night.

After the oooing and awing finally subsided, I began explaining about all of the badges the boys had earned to get to the "Arrow of Light". Calling the boys up to the campfire one at a time, everything went flawlessly. I began to start the closing ceremony when I realized I had forgotten to present the award to my own son. I was more than embarrassed. Jeff took it in stride, but I saw it in his eyes, they were sad, I had hurt his feelings. We called him up, made some silly comment about the situation and presented his award.

A few weeks later Jeff and I were working on his Pinewood Derby car for the big Cub Scout annual races. We were together in the back yard, one on one working diligently to get it just right. He was explaining to me why red, white, and blue were the best colors for his car. I turned, looked down at him and I saw it in his eyes, they were shining, all he ever cared about was simply being with me. Looking back at my actions in trying to do what I thought was best for my children, I probably neglected them more than I helped them. I wish I had those days back. I would do things a little differently, but wouldn't we all.

FISHING WITH RAYBURN

By: Jim Ferguson

I've written a couple of short stories on frogging and hunting ducks which detailed just being with some good friends or some of the tight spots I've gotten myself into.

I started fishing with Rayburn Bell back in the seventies. We also hunted quite a bit but it may not be a good idea to relate some of those stories. However, I will tell you about some of the good times he and I had while we fished together. Our first fishing adventures were fishing for catfish on the Mississippi River out from Portageville near the old ferry landing. From there we moved forward to fishing for crappie and bass on the area lakes and river chutes.

One of our most productive fishing adventures happened on Labor Day weekend in 1977. The reason the date is easy to remember is because it was the second anniversary of the Gideon Hometown Reunion. We were fishing on Wappapello Lake and staying at the Holiday Landing Resort. Rayburn had bought an old cab-over-camper for his truck and we were staying in it. Since I had worked off midnights that morning, it was noon before we got there and put everything up and managed to get the boat into the water. We headed down the lake to Caldwell Creek where we fished for an hour or so but only caught a few fish. Then I hooked into one while we were fishing in six to eight foot of water. When it bit, of course I knew it wasn't a crappie because it almost jerked the pole out of my hand. I was using a fly rod with six pound test line and it was being tested to the limit. At the first bite, I thought I might have hooked into a nice catfish. It took another ten minutes before I saw what I had--a large carp. Then it was another twenty minutes before Rayburn and I were able to get it into the boat. After guessing for a few minutes on how much it weighed, we decided to run back up the lake to the boat landing to weigh it. It topped the scales at 23 pounds. After releasing the carp we continued on with our fishing. Along the main channel we got to fishing in some moss. Now this moss wasn't the type that just grew up like a mat. Rather, it was a spiraling type that was easy to fish without getting hung up. Because the crappies were there, we fished up and down the lake for the next three days in the different moss beds that we found. By the time we loaded up to go home on Monday we had caught 634 head of fish--the most fish I've ever caught in such a short period of time! After we got home and put our fish into the freezer, Rayburn called Cleo Pattilo. The two of them went back and fished the rest of the week. Now all of our fishing trips weren't that productive, but we still always had a great time.

On another trip to the lake Rayburn and I were bass fishing in Possum Creek. Bass fishing was something we only did when nothing else was biting. On this particular day the wind was blowing pretty hard. For those of you who did not know Rayburn, he was a big man. He had put on his life jacket which would not snap in front. While fishing the shore line Rayburn got a good bite and when he went to set the hook...out the side of the boat he went! Now if you haven't ever seen a big man who is wearing a life jacket that will not snap in front fall out of the boat, you have missed a sight! Since the life jacket came up around his arms, the only way he could swim was to dog paddle. And I, being the good fishing buddy that I was, laughed until I hurt during the entire time he was asking for help. When I was finally able to control the laughter, I told him to just go ahead and stand up and get back into the boat because the water wasn't as deep as he thought. It took a while but he finally laughed about it too.

Now I'll tell on myself. We had been fishing most of the morning but hadn't caught many fish and hadn't seen anyone else on the lake. We were discussing the situation when Rayburn came up with the idea that since it was so hot we needed to know where the thermal line was. The thermal line is the area where the hot water and the cold water meet. If you have ever swam in a lake you probably have felt it. Since I was hot any way and no one else was around, I stripped out of my clothes and over the side I went. Now no sooner had I hit the water than I realized a boat was coming up the lake. You would think that it would go on past us since they had the whole lake to fish but, NO, they didn't. They stayed right there in our area. It was a man, his wife, and two kids. They pulled to a stop within forty yards of us and started blue gill fishing. Now Rayburn, not being one to pass up a chance for a little laughter at my expense, started talking to them! There I am naked as the day I was born and hanging onto the back side of the boat while fervently hoping they could not see me. I whispered to him to take the trolling motor and move on away from them so I could get back in the boat. But again not wanting to miss a chance to laugh, he says in a loud voice, "Come on; get back in the boat; and let's leave this place for them." He did however leave in a few minutes and the people were none the wiser as to my predicament.

Rayburn and I continued to fish and hunt for many more years together and shared a lot of good times and memories--more than I'd have time to write. My dear friend died in November of 2001 and is missed by all who knew him. I thank him for the memories.

IN MEMORY OF RAYBURN BELL

A FROGGING TRIP

By: Jim Ferguson

Geez, it's been another hot night at work but it usually is this time of year. First day of July and it is midnight; I probably should be going on home this time of night but, living by my standards, I work hard and play hard. Tonight it's time to play. I'm meeting a friend of mine on the floodway ditches tonight. I'll see what the boy is made of. I ran into him early today and while we were talking about frogging, he mentioned he would like to go. He's never been before so here we are.

After he helped me unload the gigs from the truck and check our lights, I explained to him how this would work. I told him since the ditch was so low we couldn't float a boat, we would be wading. We would wade down the ditch shining our lights on the west bank a foot or so above the waters edge. The reason we would shine to the west bank was because the moon was still rising in the east and the frogs would be facing the moon and on our return trip we would shine them on the east bank because by then the moon would be farther over in the sky.

So with all the formalities over, we put on our wading shoes and hit the ditch. I have to admit the boy didn't back up a bit; he stayed right behind me like an old pro. Now for you folks reading this... if you have never been frogging I don't really know how to explain it to you. There is just something about being out at night on a dark ditch with the frogs croaking and the bugs a buzzin'-- no better therapy for a country boy. It just puts one's mind right at ease.

We hadn't gone far when the ole bull frog we had heard croaking while we were getting ready to go came into view. Showing the frog to Steve I told him, "Now is the time to see you do your stuff, boy. Stick him! To my surprise he stuck that ole bull frog just like a pro and I have to admit I was a little disappointed. I was hoping to get a good laugh out of his missing it.

And that is how the night went as we went down the ditch spotting the frogs. Steve and I taking turns sticking them. Things went good-- we talked, laughed, even told a few jokes.

We were almost to our turning around point to head back to the bridge and trucks when I noticed Steve was standing still several yards behind me. As I turned and shined my light his way I saw the problem. A snake was between us swimming on top of the water toward Steve. He asked what he should do now. I saw that it was just a water snake (non-poisonous) and I told him not to worry about it. If it got too close to just splash a little water at it and it would go on its way. Now if that would actually work or not I didn't know but seemed to be the best thing at the time to tell him. Well I was right proud of that boy at that time! He never lost his cool and continued on down the ditch where I was standing. He even splashed water toward the snake and it worked because the snake left. Well it went under so I guess it left as we didn't see it any more.

After making the turn we returned to the truck and gigging several more frogs on the way. We put our things up, put on our dry shoes, cleaned our frogs, and headed on into town. By that time it was early in the morning and the sky was getting light in the east. We said our good nights and I thanked him and he thanked me for taking him. He said he had a blast and would love to go again. A day or two later I cooked those frogs and had Steve come over to help me eat them while we talked about that night and made plans to go again thinking next time we would take his dad.

I know Steve had a good time that night and maybe even learned something. I know I did: I learned that Steve would be a man you could ride the river with. In this case, wade the ditch.

In Memory of Steve Evans

HANG ON, SON

By: Jim Ferguson

In the process of my writing these stories and you folks reading them, you know a lot of them have been about the things I have done and the trouble I have gotten myself into. I have been thrown, fallen and pushed out of boats, wrecked three- and four-wheelers, suffered all kinds of injuries from bicycles, and been almost run over by trains (which is another story I'll have to tell you about some other time). You have learned about some of the people whom I've known in my life who were important to me. Unfortunately some of the trouble and mishaps that I brought about didn't just include me but, as was often the case, there were other innocent people involved. It was just their bad luck to be with me when one of my "great ideas" turned out to be "not-so-great" an idea. One of these unfortunate souls is my son, Adam. For those of you who know me, you know that I am like most parents: I would do anything in this world for my kids. I would gladly lay down my life for them to have one more day upon this earth, and I would <u>never</u> knowingly do anything that would harm them in any way. But on some of our excursions, there has been a time or two that the possibility of one of the boys being injured did arise. This particular event took place on one of our many family fishing trips. For several days I had been fishing at Point Pleasant which is a chute off the Mississippi River near Portageville, Missouri. Because I had caught some really nice blue gills, when Saturday came around we loaded up the boat, packed a lunch, and headed that way. Launching our boat into the Mississippi River we ran upstream for a mile entering the Point Pleasant chute through a ditch on the south end and worked our way north through the willows until we reached the area where I had been catching the blue gill the last few days. After taking a few minutes to get the poles sorted out and the hooks baited with crickets, the boys were soon catching some really nice blue gill. The good thing about catching blue gill is when they are on the spawning beds, you can catch large numbers of them and catch them as fast as you can bait your hook and that is exactly what my boys were doing. As the morning wore on, the wind began to blow really hard making it difficult for me to keep the boat in one place even with aid of a trolling motor. I was having a hard time maintaining our position but was managing to do so until Lyle broke the hook off his line while trying to get a fish loose that had wrapped itself around one of the trees trunks underwater. While I was tying a new hook on Lyle's line I asked Adam, who was sitting in the back of the boat, to hang on to a tree to keep us from being blown away from our blue gill "honey hole." Now there is something you should know: Although Adam wasn't over seven or eight years old at this time he was a very strong little boy for his age and size. He could do push ups and sit ups until you got tired of counting them. In fact during one of our visits to a local fair in Kennett, Missouri, the Marines had a booth set up and were challenging the older boys to see if they were fit enough for the Marines. As we passed the booth, Adam (who was only six or seven years old at the time), walked up to the Marines and challenged them. At first they humored him. After he had completed fifty push ups, they all took notice. By the time he topped a hundred, they were amazed that a boy of his age could do so many. When we left the booth they were in awe of Adam's ability. Not only did he do over a hundred push ups, but he then rolled over on his back and knocked out a lot of set ups and continued to do several pull ups. Before we left the booth, they told him to come back when he was older because the country could certainly use strong men like him. With that in mind you understand why I thought nothing of asking him to hold on to the tree while I tied the hook on Lyle's line. Before I finished tying the hook, I heard Adam holler, "Hey, Dad! Help!" Looking up I saw Adam doing what I had asked him to do--he was hanging on to the tree. In fact he was bear hugging it. The problem was that he was no longer in the boat but, rather, was twenty feet behind us and the wind was quickly blowing us further away from him. Seeing this I laid Lyle's pole down and as quickly as possible turned the boat around, went back, and got Adam into the boat again. After I tied the boat to a tree, we laughed about it while we ate our lunch. We continued to catch blue gill and Adam caught one of the biggest blue gill I have ever seen. Later that evening we decided we had all the fish we wanted to clean and headed home with yet another great memory in our hearts. And as always, time passes and changes all things. The boys grew up and left us with the memories of our lives. To this day, we still tell this story. Nowadays though when I ask Adam to do something, he will often (quite rightly, I might add) ask me, "Dad, are you sure this is a good idea?"

Thanks for the memory, Adam!

Love, DAD

KITES, JUNE BUGS, AND BIRDS

By: Jim Ferguson

Living on the farm did in fact have its disadvantages. During the summer when school wasn't in session, we would go for weeks without going to town other than attending church on Sundays, Sunday nights, and Wednesday nights. We did take advantage of the chance to slip out between training union and church to place rocks underneath the gas pedals of the cars in the parking lot because it was always fun to watch someone trying to leave church and not being able to gain speed until they stopped and removed the rock. I didn't come up with this trick on my own; I suspect it has been passed down for generations. Telephones weren't used by kids back then as they are today so we were left out of the loop as to what the city or town kids were doing for entertainment. However it did afford us the opportunity to expand our minds when it came to finding ways to have fun. There was always the fishing to be done in the surrounding ditches or building forts or digging small caves or camping out while playing on the ditch berm. On rainy days we could go to the barn and play hide and seek or have a good old corn cob fight if enough neighbor kids came over to play. However as enjoyable as these things were, we often got bored and were always looking for other forms of entertainment. One of the things we often did was fly kites. The practice of kite flying goes way back in time and not just by kids. I remember how excited we would get in the spring of the year when kite flying was at its best. We would often make our own but occasionally we would get a store-bought kite. Having spent many afternoons flying kites, I learned a few tricks. For instance, you need a slight breeze. If the wind was blowing too hard you usually couldn't get the kite up into the air. If you did, it would soon be slammed back to the earth which often broke the kite. But on those perfect days, you could fly your kite for hours. Quite often we left them staked out and let them fly all night. We also learned you could take a piece of paper with a small hole in it and attach it to the string of the kite. The vibration and wind would force the note up to the kite. We called that "sending a note to the kite." We also learned to fly them into each other but that usually ended in tearing up the kites so we didn't do that very often--especially with store-bought kites.

As spring faded and summer advanced, we would change from kites to June bugs. A June bug is a hard-shelled bug about the size of your thumb from the last knuckle to the end of your nail and is green in color. In order to fly a June bug, you need to tie a length of string just behind the bug's head. Be sure to place the knot on the underneath side. Every day string will do but the lighter the string the better because the weight of the string has an effect on the distance and the amount of air time you get out of the bug before it tires. With butcher's string, the bug can fly ten feet high or so but not much further. Lightweight fishing line (two pound test or less) allows the bug to get as high as twenty feet as well as stay aloft longer. My cousins from up north (city kids) were always amazed with this, and we were always proud to show off for them.

Now if you read the title of this story, it's not going to take much imagination on your part to guess where this story is headed. Bingo! Give yourself a cigar! We are going to fly birds by utilizing much the same method as flying June bugs. Since we lived in the country where there were plenty of barns, there was always a good supply of birds to be caught. Catching birds is a little harder, of course, than catching June bugs. June bugs could always be caught at night. Being attracted to the light, they would gather around the outside windows of the house. The best way and time to catch the birds was also at night. All that was needed was a flashlight and a fishing dip net. The best location was the barn. Just shine the light in the barn until you find some birds roosting, and simply climb within reach of the birds while ensuring the light remains focused on their eyes. To get the best results, it takes two people: one to shine the light and the other person to grab the bird by hand or catch it with the net if it should fly off the roost. After the bird is captured, the rest is a piece of cake. Make a harness out of string and tie it to the bird making certain it is tight enough the bird won't slip out. Then tie your flight string to the harness and you are in the bird flying business. I would like to mention that after trying several types of birds, I found the pigeon to be the best flyer since it is stronger than sparrows or other small birds. The longer the string you have for flying birds, the better off you are. I always liked tying them to my fishing pole with lots of line, but it does take a lot of practice to get them to circle and not just to fly away. Getting the bird back in is often extremely hard and generally ends with their getting tired and just landing. Time passes and changes all things. I grew up and left my childhood entertainment behind. I began thinking the only way to have fun was by buying the latest toy or newest boat or fishing pole. But my advice to you is this: the next time someone tells you to "go fly a kite" think instead "Flying birds is more of a challenge."

GROCERY MONEY

By: Terry Weldon

From the time I was about ten years old til about fifteen years old it was my job to bring home the grocery money. That seems a little young for being the bread winner, well here is how I did it.

My Grandpa P.O. Beasley was a hard working sharecropper all of his life and his boss never had to tell him when to be at work and when to quit. It was simple for him, if the sun was up, you should be at work, if the Gideon Box Plant whistle blew, it was five o'clock and he went home. Even a half mile away with the tractor running you could hear that whistle. Grandpa worked five and a half days a week on the farm and I never saw him take a drink of anything but water while at work and mostly sweet tea at home. However, come Saturday at noon, he would park that tractor in the corner of the yard, go in the house, take a bath, take off his dirty overalls and put on a clean pair. (Why call them a pair of overalls when they were one piece?). By the time he was finished and dressed, I would have his shaving mug and razor ready on the front porch where I gave him a nice clean shave for fifty cents. This would get me in the Malden theater and get me popcorn and a sodie.

After Grandpa was shaven he headed for down town Gideon Missouri, particularly, Gibb's Bar. Upon entering Gibb's he would walk straight to the bar where Gibbs would hand him two half pints of Colonel Lee whisky. He would open one and drink down in one gulp and slip the second bottle in his back pocket. Then he would go out to the front of Gibb's to sit with the other elderly gentlemen of the town on what we called "Spit and Whittle Corner". There were steps at the entrance of the Bar with an eight foot benches on both sides of the steps. Both benches were usually full by this time.

The activities going on at these benches were somewhat less than honest when it came to "knife swapping". No not "Wife Swapping"; that was the next generation! For some unknown reason this generation thought one of the rights to manhood was to have the sharpest knife in town. I was always amazed by the fact that each man on those benches had at least two knives on him at any given time, one to show how sharp he could make it, and the other to swap. Now, here is how the swapping took place. First, two gentlemen would bring out the knife they had been sharpening for ten minutes, (every man on that bench had his own whit rock in his pocket to sharpen his knives), for you city folk, that was a small sharpening stone. Anyway, both gentlemen interested in swapping knives would first show how sharp his knife was by shaving the hair on his arm, not all of the hair, just enough to prove his point. Just looking at the old men's arms was pretty funny with several patches of hair shaved off on all of them. OK, Back to the swap. If either one of the men had to scrap the knife blade more than once to remove the patch of hair, the other gentleman got the choice of swapping or not. For example, you scrapped the patch of hair on your arm and it came off nice and clean, however I had to scrap twice, you won the right to decide if you wanted to swap knives after you presented them to each other. Right along here Grandpa would stop to take a "break". He would go back into the bar, walk through and out the back door to what was known as the "Bull Pen". No, there were no baseball players warming up and no bulls back there either, even though it did smell like it most of the time.

The bull pen was the back yard for the bar and it had a privacy fence on both sides running back to the side walls of Dye's barber shop. The only way in or out of the bull pen was through Gibb's bar. This area was extremely important to the bar's patrons because Gibb's had no restroom. Therefore, this is where the gentlemen "relieved" themselves. So, Grandpa went to the edge of the porch and, well, you get the picture…

It had been about thirty minutes since Grandpa had chugged the first half pint. When he was finished with "his business", he took the bottle from his back pocket, opened it and down it went in maybe two gulps. He would stop and purchase two more half pints, one for each back pocket, on his way back to the bench out front.

Now every man on spit and whittle corner new there was going to be a "swap" and they were all paying close attention to this event. Once the decision was made as to who could say yes or no to the knife swap, the two gentlemen would put those knives back in their pocket because they would never swap their sharp knives. They would reach in the other pocket, pull out a "swapping" knife, keeping it palms down so the other gentlemen cannot see it. Both gents dropped their knife into the other ones hand at the same time. Most of the time, these two knives weren't worth ten cents. Most were rusty, handles missing or blades broken, may have been one they found in the field where it had been buried for twenty years. That was the fun of the knife swapping game. To see who could come up with the worst knife and pawn it off on some other sucker. The sharp knife competition had nothing to do with it whatsoever!

Now another thirty minutes has passed and Grandpa has felt the "urge" again to visit the bull pen. This time he chugs his third half pint, then takes care of his business. There were usually two or three other fellas in the bull pen feeling no pain at this point in the day. Grandpa would sit down on the back steps and shoot the breeze with one or two of them, by this time the conversations were not very coherent on either side and after a few minutes both men would fall silent, lean back against the wall to soak in the afternoon sunshine. They were already pretty warm on the inside, now the outside was getting there and the sandman was right behind them sprinkling fairy dust all over the back porch of Gibb's bar.

This is where I came in. My job, per Granny Beasley, was to go through Grandpa's billfold and take all of his money but three dollars. I was usually next door at Dye's pool hall or the City Café. I knew he was about ripe for the picking so I would go down to Gibb's, walk to the back porch where I would find him "enjoying" the afternoon. Because Grandpa wore overalls, it was easy to access his billfold simply by unsnapping the bib and taking the billfold out, never waking him. Usually this would be perceived as theft in most parts of the country, however, everyone in town new exactly what I was doing and no one ever said a word. Truth be told, I probably wasn't the only boy doing this behind Gibbs on a Saturday afternoon. Making sure I took all but three dollars, I would take the rest home to Granny Beasley because it was my job to bring home the Grocery money. Not exactly what you expected when you began reading this, was it?

LABOR DAY REUNIONS

By: Jim Ferguson

Once again Labor Day has approached and, once again and as often as my work would allow, I attended the Labor Day Reunion in Gideon, Missouri. The reunion was first held in 1976 the same year as the bicentennial of this nation. In the early years of the reunion I was a young adult who had only been out of school six years. Thirty-five years after that, I've became one of the younger "old timers" attending the event. I have always found it enjoyable to attend because it gives me a chance to reconnect with classmates or friends I haven't seen in awhile. As time passes and changes the events of our lives, it was really evident this year as I wondered around the school and school grounds. I came to the realization that most of the people who were my parents' age are no longer here but have passed on. Most of the people my age are now having grandchildren show up which is a scary fact that means we are now becoming the older group. That brings into play another amazing thing--how we are becoming more and more like our parents not only in actions but also in looks. I was surprised at the number of men and women I saw who look like their moms or their dads did when they were the same age a few years ago. Case in point: after spending a few hours on the school grounds my wife, Brenda, and Holly Fielder, a friend of ours, went to the Community Center (the old Ben Franklin store) where Holly's family was having a family reunion. While there I met and visited several members of her family--most of whom I had known my entire life. However I did meet one of Holly's cousins, Helen

Marchbanks. I was taken aback. Looking at her face and into her eyes was like looking back into time twenty-five years ago. Her resemblance to her father was amazing! It was like seeing an old friend again. Helen's dad was Burl Fielder who was also known as Shorty by friends and family.

Burl and my dad became acquainted in the forties when they both moved to the Peach Orchard/Wardell, Missouri area. Burl ran a pool hall. Playing pool and baseball were two of the favorite activities for the men at that time. With my dad being a lover of both games, he and Burl soon got to know each other and stayed friends for life. They often hunted and fished together in their early years. I remember once while I was probably in my early teens, Dad and I went deer hunting and were staying in an old farm house Allen Richardson had on a hill farm close to Van Buren. Burl was there, too, along with several other men. When it got close to bed time Burl gave a thirty minute warning to all that he was ready for bed. The reason for the warning was Burl was the "snoringest" man I've ever been around. If you weren't asleep before he fell asleep, odds were you weren't going to get any sleep. That night he lived up to his reputation. Dad and I slept in the cab of the truck the next night. A few years later I became a fan of the game of pool, too, and played many games of pool with Burl. Although he was well up in years by that time, he was a hard man to beat in a game of eight ball--even with cataracts covering his eyes.

In closing, I would like to suggest you go to your school or family reunions if you haven't done so.

You may see a long-time friend in the face of someone you didn't know.

Thanks for the memories, Helen.

LEAVING SIGNS

By: Jim Ferguson

Long before the atlas was printed or GPS was developed, men have been leaving signs of their passing. I suspect from the time man first walked away from his cave and started wandering the Earth, he has been leaving signs either to find his way back home or for the purpose of making it easy for others to follow. Signs have been found in caves, on stone tablets along the coast, and all over North America dating long before Columbus came across the ocean claiming to have found a new land thus proving that Columbus was really a "Johnny come lately." Now it has been said by some who know me that I am not far removed from the cave myself. I'd say that if leaving a sign is a sign of that then I will be forced to agree with them. As far back as I can remember I have been leaving signs of my passing. This dates as far back to the days that I rode my stick horse across the fields or along the dusty roads on the farm. I was forever stopping on my journeys and leaving signs by either drawing something on the ground or by taking my pocket knife and marking a tree. Marking trees was used by the Indians as well as by frontiersmen as they explored the new world. It is something I still do today if I am in woods that are new to me where I could become lost. As you have heard me say several times, time changes all things.

But there is one exception. Even as I have aged I still leave signs. I have traveled across the United States and across the oceans and have left signs of my passing every where I've been. I have also passed this down to my sons. As we traveled on vacation when they were young, we always left signs of our being there. We often did this by simply placing four rocks stacked on top of each other. This became our family symbol. We have left signs from the Smoky Mountains to Texas to Yellowstone to the Black Hills. In addition we have also left signs at the Grand Canyon and in campgrounds all across Missouri, Arkansas, and Tennessee. I became aware of passing this down to my sons for the first time while we were fishing. On this trip we had taken one of their young friends by the name of Eric McCain with us. After we had spent several hours in the boat, they became restless so I pulled on to the bank and allowed the boys to run and stretch their legs for a while. After twenty minutes or so, I decided I'd best go looking for them. As I made my way down the logging road they took off on I came to a cross roads and there it was: an arrow made out of sticks pointing to the direction they went. This assured me I was doing something right and they were learning how to find their way in the woods. We have left signs at friends homes when we dropped by and they were not at home. To do this we would simply place something in front of the door. Once I did this and when they returned home, the wife wondered out loud how the broom got in front of the door. Her husband told her, "Well Jim has been here." Of course she asked him, "Now how do you know that?" His response was, "He is the only one I know who still leaves signs."

Since that day he has left signs at my door also and we always know.

Leaving signs can be a blessing. I would like to tell you about a sign I came across that is very dear to my heart and that made the lifetime habit of leaving signs worth it all. For those of you who know me, you know that I lost my oldest son Lyle due to a work accident several years ago. A few months after he had passed away, his brother and I were out shooting our guns at Three Ditch Bridge south of Gideon, Missouri. After shooting several rounds we were preparing to leave when I saw it. Carved into the edge of the bridge was "FERGI," the name both of my sons and I have been called short for Ferguson. Upon seeing it, I asked Adam if he had ever carved his name in this bridge and he told me no. I then said, "Well you need to see this. Your brother left us a sign. A day or so later I mentioned it to my stepdaughter Karen. In turn she then mentioned it to her husband Jeff. Since he was aware the bridge was going to be replaced within a few weeks, he decided to retrieve that small section of wood that had the name "FERGI" carved into it. With help from his brother, Justin, he gave it to me that Christmas. One of the best Christmas gifts I have ever received! Karen gave me a very special gift that year also. She gave me a grandson whom she named Jeffery Lyle after both her husband and stepbrother. So as you travel down this path of life I suggest to you that you leave your sign whether it be a rock placed somewhere or sticks laid upon a path. Or it can be done simply by touching someone's life in a positive way such as a kind word, a helping hand, or anything else that will leave a sign of your having passed this way.

Thanks for the memories.

I SMELL A SNAKE

By: Terry Weldon

I have a cousin, Freddie Layne, who swore he could smell a snake if one was anywhere around us. Of course, we thought he was a little silly at the time, but one July night in 1966 he made a believer out of me and several other cousins that were with us. The family had all gathered over at my cousin Sonny Kilgo's house near Risco Missouri for some special family event. I can't remember what it was, but like most people in Southeast Missouri, we didn't need much of a reason to get together and eat.

After supper there were several cousins out in the backyard swatting mosquitoes and telling tales when Fred came up with the fact that he could smell a snake if it were in his local area. We all had a good laugh. I told them if I were with Sonny Kilgo I knew if there was a snake near us because I could smell Sonny, cause he liked them as much as I do!

I, for one, am petrified of snakes, doesn't matter what kind they are, how big or small they are, I simply can't handle them. There were a few cousins that had no fear of them at all, but most were as scared of them as I am.

It was nearing sunset that evening and we were snooping around in Uncle Cecil Kilgo's tractor shed where we found about fifteen to twenty fishing poles all wadded in the corner. We picked out the one we wanted to fish with, took it outside, cleaned it a little, threw it out a few times to make sure the fishing line was still good.

Living out in the country, Uncle Cecil had the drain for his kitchen sink and washing machine draining just passed his back yard. As all men from that are knew that was the perfect place to dig up fishing worms. A couple of cousins were digging us up some bait while the others got the poles ready. We walked down the gravel road to number four ditch bridge to see if we could catch a few catfish. The bridge was an old iron rail bridge that looked like a railroad trestle with board runners for the cars to cross over on. We lined up on the bridge and dropped our lines in the ditch and went back to telling our tales. It was just about dark and after a minute or two someone caught a nice catfish. There were about six of us fishing and not one thought to bring a fish stringer. Fred tramples off down the ditch bank. You couldn't have paid me to go down there. He stirred around in the weeds and reached down to bring up some sort of heavy vine, fashioned a stringer and strung up the catfish, staked it out on the bank and just sat down right there in the weeds. I said, "let me know if you smell any snakes down there", we all had a laugh and kept fishing. After a minute or two Fred shouted up to us to shine the flashlight down his way in the ditch, that he smelled a snake. We shined the light in the middle of the ditch and sure enough, there was a snake swimming down the ditch. We laughed and said in this particular ditch you could see a snake every minute if you looked around. There were another couple of catfish caught up on the bridge and of course, me being the smallest of the group, I had to take it down for Fred to add it to the stringer. Reluctantly, I eased down the back with one eye watching the path I was walking on and the other eye doing a 360 degree look around the snake infested area.

There were a few more catfish caught and I decided to just sit down with Fred and let someone else bring them down to us. Fred turned to me and said, "I smell another one". I was becoming a believer, so I stood up, shined the light around and there it was on the other bank slithering up into the weeds. At this point, if Fred were an evangelist, I would have started sending him money!

As darkness fell upon us and the fish were beginning to quit biting, we just talked and teased each other for a while longer, (one of those great times you look back on and were just glad you were there). The mosquitoes had found out where we were and we were all starting to look like we had chicken pox. Just as we were talking about going back to the house, Fred said, "Boys I smell a snake and he is close"! Well, me being a devout believer, I shined the light all over that ditch bank, but could see nothing. Fred insisted it was close and I wasn't doubting him for a second. I suggested we get the fish and head back. He grabbed the stringer and brought out a nice stringer of 8 to 10 catfish, of which the one on the bottom of the stringer had a nice water moccasin hanging on it. Fred, being one of those that didn't fear snakes, reached down and grabbed that snake behind the head, pulled it off that catfish and said, "here, hold this"!

I had just finished a plate of peach cobbler when the rest of them got back to the house! Fred said, "I meant hold the stringer".

MUD TATERS, CORN, AND CRAWDAD ON A STICK

By: Jim Ferguson

Having been called out earlier today to help remove some of the larger fish in the Diversion Channel that have been feeding on the smaller pan fish, I am happy to report it was a successful day. I was able to catch and remove several gars. With their long snoots and razor-sharp teeth, they are very lethal killers who will eat several times their own body weight in a days' time. However, like everything else, they do have a purpose in the system of things in the world. Since they will eat anything that is dead in the water, they help maintain the ecosystem and that is fine. But the problem is they also feed on small pan fish like crappie and blue gill which are two of my favorite fish to catch. So naturally when the chance to remove a few of these notorious killers arises I always take advantage of it. Now I know this doesn't put me in the same class as other super heroes but it does make me feel good knowing that sometimes I can make a difference in the lives of the small fry. Sometimes I have the feeling they know that someone is looking out for them. Take this morning, for instance. While removing a large gar from the water I saw a small crappie rise to the top of the water, turn on his side, and lift a fin in a waving motion as though he was telling me thanks. As the day continued I soon began to realize that although I had gotten an early start it was now beginning to warm up and, with a light, hot, dry wind blowing, I was soon noticing the effects of it. Fortunately for me I did take soft drinks and water to keep me hydrated but the one thing I forgot to bring along was some lunch. Looking into the cooler of my boat I realized I must have eaten all of my stash of peanut butter and crackers that I normally have there. Now that set me to thinking about what I would have done under these circumstance when I was young. The answer to that is I would have made do with what I could catch or find. Living in the country as I did there was always something I could find to eat. Be it a nearby turnip patch, cornfield, or a garden to raid, food was always there. I could also always catch a fish or crawdad, build me a fire, and cook them on a stick over the open flame. Now I will have to say that fish, rabbits, and other fare cooked this way isn't as good as it would be fried up with a little salt and pepper--but it is edible. Now crawdads are pretty tasty and are similar to cooking shrimp on a bbq grill. Add them to a couple of other items such as an ear of corn still in the shuck straight from the field. This type of corn is a lot bigger than sweet corn. Add a potato and you will have one of the best meals ever cooked over an open fire. Now I'm sure there are several boy scouts and girl scouts out there who have eaten mud taters but for those who haven't I'll explain how you fix them. Take an ordinary baking potato and coat it with mud (gumbo works really well) at least a quarter-inch thick making sure to cover the entire potato. Then simply place it beside a good fire or cover it with hot coals allowing it to bake. When the mud is dry and starts to crack, the potato will be done and ready to eat. Just knock the mud away and the peeling will protect the tater from the dirt. Cooking the ear of corn is done the same way you would cook it on your bbq grill: leave it in the shuck, lay it close to the fire or on the coals, and turn often. (I always like soaking mine in water--ensuring the shuck is good and wet seems to help steam the corn.) For the main course of the meal you need some good, big crawdads which could always be found during the spring and summer. Now if you had a rake you could always rake them out of the ditch but if no simply walk along the water's edge until you find a crawdad hole. Place a string or a rag into the hole and the crawdad would latch a claw onto it. Then all you had to do was ease him out or, if it was a big enough hole, you could run your finger down into it allowing him to clamp his claw onto your finger. After gathering a dozen or so of these, cut several small sticks and sharpen a point on them just as though you were roasting marshmallows. Place your crawdads on the stick. Be sure to place them so they would lean out over your fire and let them roast. Now you can do this two ways: whole or just the tails. I always liked cooking them whole myself but some people don't care so much about cooking and eating the whole thing. So there you have it--a meal fit for a king and a lot cheaper than eating at Red Lobster. Give this a try the next time you are on a camping trip with your kids or grandkids. You will have a great meal as well as some great memories!

MY LAST FLIP

By: Jim Ferguson

In a couple of my stories you have heard me speak of Wilburn, Arkansas, where my mother was raised. It is situated right in the foothills of the Ozarks, a beautiful part of the country. When I was a young boy, our family often travelled there to visit Granny and Grandpaw and always had a great time playing in the creeks and on the hillsides. Yes, great times and great memories were made there!

Located a few miles from Wilburn is Heber Springs, Arkansas--a beautiful and quaint old town. I remember going there quite a bit while visiting the grandparents. The local drug store still featured a soda fountain and sold sodas, ice cream floats, or just ice cream in a cone. On the way from Wilburn to Heber Springs, we would cross one of the nation's few remaining swinging bridges. This one-lane bridge spanned the Little Red River. I remember actually seeing the bridge rise and fall every time we drove across. As we approached town there was a single hill, called Sugar Loaf Mountain, rising several hundred feet in the middle of a big flat area. We often climbed to the top which offered a great view of the surrounding area. In the early sixties the Corps of Engineers built a large dam across The Little Red River forming a huge lake which was named Greers Ferry Lake. President John F Kennedy dedicated it in the fall of 1963 just three months before he was killed in Dallas, Texas. As one would expect, after the lake was built our summer trips to Granny's house began to include trips to the lake for swimming. Now let me explain a little something about this lake. It is a deep, clear lake. I have run my boat across it using sonar and have found the water to be anywhere from 100 to 180 feet deep in places and some of those place are along the shoreline. Part of the shoreline is made of sheer cliffs which are just perfect for diving since they range in height from5 feet to 50-60 feet. As you know I have always been one looking for adventure so it didn't take too long before I was jumping and diving off the highest cliffs. By the time I was sixteen I was doing back flips off the fifty footers and I will tell you for sure that is a true rush. On one of our trips to the lake my cousin-- Bill Cooper, my brother, and I were diving off the tallest ones when my youngest sister, Karma, decided she, too, was old enough to get in on the fun. Since she was only eight or nine years old at the time, I would only allow her to jump, not dive, from the 50 foot cliffs. After a few false starts, she soon managed to gather the nerve and off the cliff she went. Later on that day when Dad came to the cliffs to check on us, she was able to coax Dad into jumping off by telling him she would jump if he would. Of course Dad, assuming she would not have the nerve and not knowing that Karma had been jumping all afternoon, agreed to jump if she jumped. To his surprise she jumped before he could change his mind which left Dad in a really bad place. He either had to jump or lose face with his young daughter. That is the only time I ever remember Dad jumping off the cliffs. He exclaimed he went so deep he didn't think he would ever surface. As time passed, I grew up, married, and had children of my own. We continued to go to Heber Springs and Greers Ferry Lake to camp, swim, water ski, and dive off the cliffs. Enjoying adventure as much as I, my boys were diving off the cliffs at a young age. Diving off the cliffs became a rite of passage to all the boys and some of the girls. It has now been several years since I have been camping and swimming on Greers Ferry Lake. As usual on our last trip there we were boating and skiing. I anchored the boat out from the cliffs. Brenda stayed in the boat while Lyle, Adam, Karen, and I swam to the cliffs and climbed them. Upon reaching the top I began talking to some young boys who were jumping off the cliffs and asked whether they were afraid to jump saying it looked awfully high and dangerous to me. Being young and proud, they swelled their young chests out and told me there was nothing to it. While they were doing all this boasting, I slowly approached the edge of the cliff and, giving myself a huge push, I did a double back flip off the cliff. The last thing I heard before hitting the water was. "DID YOU SEE THAT OLD SON-OF-A-GUN!?" Surfacing I began swimming to the boat with Lyle, Adam, and Karen following right behind me since they had jumped after I did. We climbed into the boat, waved at the young boys, and roared off into the sunset laughing about the boys' remarks of the OLD MAN.

Yes, we have had a lot of fun on that beautiful recreational lake. It's where Brenda learned to water ski and I must say it took her many, many tries to get up. Although she was exhausted, she would not quit until she managed to get up and stay up. She was so excited and really enjoyed skiing. It was also here where she held her breath (in fear she would lose her entire family in one swell swoop as she puts it) as she watched Karen, Lyle, Adam, and me all jump simultaneously off the cliffs for the first time. She would never participate in our cliff-jumping—Brenda doesn't jump off anything!

But as always, time passes and changes all things. I have made my last flip off those cliffs and the quaint town of Heber Springs has turned into a tourist town. The valley of Sugar Loaf Mountain has been "developed" with condominiums and a junior college surrounding it. The ole swinging bridge is no longer there. It collapsed several years ago killing a couple of kids after several other kids got it to swinging. "No Diving" signs have been posted on the cliffs. But the lake is still pretty; the camping is great; there is good trout fishing below the dam; and it's a great place to visit and make some wonderful memories.

Enjoying life's memories.

LOVE THEM MULBERRIES

By: Terry Weldon

Back in the early to mid 1960s, there was a field road where our driveway was. When you turned into our driveway you could turn left into our yard or continue down to the end of the field road to a little unpainted farm house. This little farm house had old torn window dressings if any at all. There was a chicken coop and two trees in the yard, one of which was a large mulberry tree. They had no grass in the yard and there was either mulberry stains or bird droppings all over the yard.

The old gentleman that lived there then was named Jeff Waddles. His wife lived with him and I think her name was Bell, but I am not sure, you know for American men your memory is the second thing to go! He was a large man and he scared me and all my friends, just by looking at him. One day me and my cousin, Lonnie Jr Beasley were playing up and down the field road, riding our stick horses and hard as we could. He had a strawberry roan and I had an appaloosa. They were fine looking steeds and could run like the wind. We had ridden them down to the Waddles house one day and noticed there was no one home. We rode up to the house to give our horses a drink as they were all lathered up from running so hard and we could use a drink too. They had a square box built around there pump in the back yard near their back porch. There was a pan on the box for washing up in. We pumped some water in it and sat it in the yard, placed our stick horses heads in it and let them drink. He pumped while I drank and I pumped while he drank. It was crystal clear and cold well water. The kind you don't see any more in this country.

We heard and saw Mr Waddles coming home on the tractor and decided we didn't want to be seen riding our horses away from his house, so we ran to the chicken house to hide until he went in his house, then we could sneak away back home. As we started to open the coop door we frightened the chicken and they scrambled around the yard cackling. We decided that we would not be able to sneak out without doing the same thing to the chickens and that wouldn't work. We then both ran to the mulberry tree, which was easier to climb. We shimmed up the tree taking our horses with us. We climb a little more than half way up the mulberry tree by the time Mr Waddles drove into the driveway to park the tractor. We froze where we were and I am sure I was breathing about three breathes per minute and I don't think Lonnie Jr breathed at all. Mr Waddles climbed down from the tractor and dusted off his overalls from driving all day in a self made dust storm. He was stiff from sitting on that 'A' model John Deere that had very little seat cover left on it and half of the black from the steering wheel gone completely. He slowly walked over to the water pump, noticed the pan in the yard, yelled out at his wife for leaving it there. The wind might come along and blow it away into the field. He spouted that he wasn't made of money, sat the pan into the hole cutout on the box under the pump. He pumped it about half full, walked over to the back porch, picked up a cake of lye soap and towel and wash rag. He returned to the pump, unstapped the galluses on his overalls and flipped them over his shoulders, dropped the bib and pulled off his shirt. I was beginning to wonder exactly what I was going to see that evening, but he stopped there, soaped up the wash rag with the lye soap and began to wash his upper body. We were still trying to hold our breathes without being noticed. He was always yelling at us to stay out of the mulberry trees and the thought of him catching us red handed in his tree was almost more than I could wrap my head around. After he washed and dried off, he pulled the bib of his overalls up, connected the galluses and poured the pan of water out in the yard where the grassless soil sucked it up in seconds. He replaced the pan, headed for the chicken house stirred around in there for three or four minutes while Lonnie Jr and I hung on to those limbs with every muscle in our butt cheeks. Finally,

Mr Waddles came out of the chicken house with five or six eggs wrapped in the towel he just used to dry off with. As the sun was turning orange, getting ready to set, Mr Waddles stepped up on his back porch, opened the door, turned back to the Mulberry tree and shouted, "you boys get on down out of that mulberry tree and get on home before it gets dark"! Then he went on in his house to eat supper...

PAPPY

By: Jim Ferguson

There are always a lot of different people in one's life who help influence a person. They help mold you into the person you become. Your dad and mother are usually on the top of that list of people, but there are others also. Sometimes it may be a school teacher, a ball coach, a preacher, or it could just be a good man in the community who is often the one who wears the ring.

But every now and then it is someone who is most unlikely to do so. One that most people would never dream of it being. Now there were a lot of different people in my life who helped mold me. One of the men was Pappy. Pappy was an older man who lived across the road from us not more than two or three good rock throws away. Now for those who don't understand a rock throw, it is a means of measurement. You simply throw a rock and multiply the distance it travels by the number of times it takes throwing the rock to reach the distance to where you are going. This is not to be confused with a chunk. The term "chunk" was used back in the day when we were clearing new ground. After the trees were cut and the stumps removed, the roots would work their way to the top. To remove those roots, you took a team of mules or horses hooked to a wagon and went through the field picking them up. These were saved for fire wood to be used in the winter to heat the house, thus "chunking the stove." Now Pappy lived in an old sharecropper's house with faded plank board on the outside walls. He lived off his social security check and by picking up extra money working from time to time for the man who farmed the land where his house sat--a meager existence at best.

Often as a young boy I'd pass Pappy's house on my way to go fishing. On some of those occasions he would call out to me to come and sit awhile on the porch and talk. Old Pappy was a kind man who never gave anyone any trouble; he was always polite to me and others. But Pappy did have a problem. He was a wino and you could always tell when the first of the month rolled around. When he would get his check, Pappy would stay drunk until his money was gone. Many a time while passing his house, I'd see Pappy passed out on the porch or in the yard and I would always stop and help Pappy back into the chair. He would always thank me and apologize for being drunk. Now it was at those times Pappy would ask if I could catch him a fish and bring to him, or he would say, "Now if you could bring me a turtle, I'll pay you fifty cents." Old Pappy did like his turtle, especially those leather backs or soft shell as we called them. Even as much as Pappy liked his turtle, I liked that fifty cents because it was a lot of money to a boy at that time. Some of the turtles I would trap and others I would shoot with a 22 rifle. By whatever means it took, I'd always get Pappy his turtle and he would always give me the fifty cents.

As with all things in life, time passes and changes all things. I grew up and left home, and Pappy moved. But I wasn't through with Pappy yet. We would once again have our paths cross. After I spent time in the Navy I returned to southeast Missouri and went to work in a local aluminum plant. One night while returning home from work, I saw a large red glow to the south of Gideon which could only mean one thing--a house fire. As I arrived a few minutes later, the fire was dying down and there were several people standing around watching. I saw Bo Wingo who was the deputy sheriff of New Madrid County and a man I'd known most of my life. Standing with him was the chief of police of Gideon. I asked Bo who lived in the house to which he replied, "Pappy." I then asked if Pappy made it out. The Chief then blurted out, "No, the damned old drunk finally burned himself up." Now to Bo Wingo's credit, he scolded the Chief for his remark.

After the fire had died out, Bo went to his car and got a body bag. Hearing the Chief and others refuse Bo when he asked for help, I gladly volunteered to help. Bo and I went into the ashes of the house and found Pappy lying beside what was left of his bed. We gently placed him into the body bag and for the last time I helped my old friend Pappy.

Now you may wonder how Pappy, a drunk and wino, could have helped mold me. Some people may inspire you to go out and do great things in life and achieve great accomplishments. In Pappy's case he inspired me to never become a drunk. I was always careful with the amount of alcohol I drank in my life and I gave it up completely in my early twenties. But Pappy also taught me something else. It doesn't matter your standing in life--at the top or at the bottom—it's what type of person you really are that matters. Yes, Pappy was a drunk and wino, but he also was a good man and cared about people.

In memory of Pappy, R.I.P. my old friend.

IT SHOULD HAVE BEEN AN OMEN

By: Jim Ferguson

During the course of the sixty years I have been alive, there have been several times when I have gotten myself into trouble by putting my hands and fingers in places where they should not have been. It is a wonder that I still have all of them! I have cut them, smashed them, and broken them in addition to having them stung and bitten. It has always been that way from my earliest remembrance to adulthood. As recently as right before my retirement I got my fingers caught in a casting wheel. Luckily I was wearing gloves and was able to yank them out from under the wheel before it got hold of them which I am sure would have resulted in the loss of some fingers and possibly my whole arm.

Now the cause of some of these problems with my fingers was brought on by my doing such things as hogging fish by running my hand and arm into holes along the banks of ditches and rivers trying to find an ole catfish holed up under them. It wasn't really a big deal as long as it was a catfish that I found. However if it was a turtle under there, I was just asking to be bitten. Some of those turtles like to really clamp down and could even take off a finger. On other occasions I have been bitten by snakes (non-poisonous) while trying to catch them or while I was playing with them. I remember one day while in the process of robbing a bird nest in the loft of the barn I ran my hand behind a pole to get the eggs out of the pigeon's nest. I discovered I was the second robber who was visiting that nest at the time. When I reached in I was greeted with a stinging bite from a black snake that was there for his lunch. He was definitely not pleased that I was interrupting him. Being as surprised as he was, I yanked my hand back, turned loose with the other hand, and fell fifteen feet to the ground. Being the hard head that I was I caught my breath, calmed myself, went back up, and captured the snake. I still have a picture of me holding him.

Going back a few years before that I once again grabbed hold of something I shouldn't have grabbed. Deciding I wanted to raise some rabbits I bought a cage from the gospel singer and song writer, Jack Campbell. While loading the cage into our truck, I grabbed hold of a big wasp nest. Now the pain of the wasps wasn't as bad as the trouble I got into for saying a few choice words after they stung me. That is the first time my mother ever heard her little boy say such sweet things. I could go on and on telling of the times that I have had close calls but I would like to share the first two times in my life that I can remember getting my hands in bad places.

I will start with the second situation. It was "wash day" and Mom was doing laundry on the back porch using an old wringer-type washing machine. When no one was around to tell me not to do something I usually got myself into a fix. This day was no different. As the clothes were being washed I began to touch the wringer as it went around and around always managing to yank my fingers back before the wringer could get hold of them. In all cases when you play with danger enough you will have to pay the price. Of course, there was an instance when I did not yank my fingers back fast enough resulting in my having my hand and arm pulled into the wringer all the way up to my shoulder. After hearing me scream Mom got back out to the porch and stopped the washer by releasing the wringer. She then carried me to the neighbor's house (James White) who drove us to town to Dr. Hopkins' clinic to see if any bones were broken. Fortunately none were broken.

The first time I ever remember getting my hand in the wrong place I couldn't have been over four or five years of age. In fact if it had not been such a traumatic ordeal I probably would not remember it at all. I had an aunt and uncle, Barbara and Alex Lee, who lived down the road a piece from us about halfway between Hartzel and Tally on 153 Hwy. Uncle Alex just happened to always be raising things including bees. While we were visiting one day, I found myself out beside the beehive although I had been told to stay away from them. Watching the bees fly in and out of the hive was amazing to me. I soon found myself sticking my finger into the hive trying to get some of the honey. As to why these bees got as upset as they did--I don't know! I mean after all how much honey could a little boy eat? But they did. I was soon covered up with swarming bees. It seemed the more I swatted at them and the more I cried and ran, the more I got stung. Once again Mom and Aunt Barbara came to my rescue, stripping my clothes and killing the bees. One would think after being taught a lesson like that at such a young age, I would learn from it or at least recognize it for the omen it was for the things to come--but then again I did say I have always been kind of hard headed didn't I?

Great memories.

STUBBORN BOYS

By: Jim Ferguson

As most of you who have been reading my stories know, I have been fishing as far back as I can remember and you also know as my boys grew older they went with me as much as school would allow. We always had a great time and, more often than not, caught a lot of fish. This story isn't so much about the fish we caught but is more about the trip and the stubbornness of the boys. The boys I'm referring to this time are my son Lyle and his cousins, Mike Cossey and John Veatch. I always fished for crappie since it is the preferred fish for the table. However, as the boys reached their teenage years and Hank Parker, a world champion bass fisherman became popular on TV, the boys decided that we should become bass fishermen. So the process began.

In order to bass fish I had to buy completely new fishing equipment including rods, reels, and lures. After spending several afternoons teaching the boys how to use bait-casting reels and wasting several spools of line in the process because of extremely knotted bird nests, we were ready to go.

Now the outing I am going to share with you took place on Wappapello Lake. Arriving very early that morning (the theory is that bass bite best at the crack of dawn), we started fishing in Milam Creek working the bank with our spinner baits and rattle traps. Of course, each boy preferred a different colored lure and approach. If you haven't ever fished out of a sixteen foot boat with three teenage boys throwing bass lures, you have missed a treat my friend—especially with these three particular boys! When they all got together like this once a year during school vacations, it was like watching the three stooges. How we ever managed to fish without having to take someone to the emergency room for hook removal, I will never know. After catching a few small bass we moved on up the lake a mile or so to Walnut Cove and began fishing. On the fourth or fifth cast I hooked into a big bass that weighed at least six pounds. While I was fighting with the fish and shouting at the boys to grab the net which was being stood on by one of the boys, the bass broke off. This was not your typical breaking of the line. Oh, no. The fish broke my pole! All I had left in my hand was the handle. I quickly dropped a marker into the water to mark the spot where I had last seen my pole before it sank to the bottom of the lake. After we enthusiastically discussed the size of the fish, I asked Lyle to get into the water and dive to the bottom to see if he could find my rod and reel. He refused as did Mike and John. Their thinking was that it was my pole so I should be the one to go get it. Let me back up here just a little and explain something. Those boys have swam all over that lake plus no telling how far I've pulled them on skis. Never in my life had I seen them not wanting to go for a swim so I know their refusal had nothing to do with being scared of the water or what was in it. They were just being plain stubborn. So my only alternative was to do what dads always do. I threatened them with the boat paddle if they didn't get into the water and look for my rod and reel. After making several half-hearted attempts at diving down to look for my rod and reel, they all came up empty-handed. Reluctantly allowing them back into the boat, I removed my shoes and socks, emptied my pockets, and hit the water myself. Swimming to the exact spot I had marked, I dove to the bottom and came up with the rod and reel in my hand. Making my way back to the boat, I tossed them to the boys and stated, "That is how you do it." To this day Mike still says I was lucky as he laughs about that trip. I know that luck had absolutely nothing to do with it. The water where the pole sunk was at least eight feet deep but the boys never went deep enough for their bottoms to get out of my sight. The fact is they were just being stubborn and not really looking for it.

And as always, time passes and changes all things. The boys grew up. Mike lives here in Jackson and is the head engineer for a big radio broadcasting company and we see each other quite often. John lives in Florida and is a cop. Another scary thought.

We lost Lyle a few years later--something I've never recovered from. As I look back upon those years we bass fished, I will always cherish them. It was always fun and are great memories today. Thanks boys. I love you all.

SWIMMING WITH THE ALLIGATORS

By: Jim Ferguson

For the last couple years I've been going to Lake Washington which is south of Greenville, Mississippi. It's an old oxbow off of the Mississippi River and is about seven miles long and one-half to three-quarters of a mile wide. On the west shore it is full of old cypress trees and cypress knees which make good spawning beds for crappie and blue gill. The water depth runs from inches next to the bank to four to five feet on the outer edges of the cypress trees. On the southern end of the lake the trees are covered with Spanish moss which gives the area an eerie look in the early morning hours and the late afternoon.

This year Joe Ward, an ole fishing buddy from Blytheville Arkansas, and my son-in-law, Jeff Crane, tagged along with me for a week of fishing for crappie. We had pretty weather this year and had managed to catch several fish--not up to our expectations but still some nice fish. On about the third or fourth day of our fishing trip, Joe and I were fishing out of his boat while Jeff was fishing out of his boat. We decided we would split up to search for better fishing places. Joe and I would head south and Jeff would fish the upper end and middle part of the lake. Plans were to meet for lunch on the lake and decide where we would fish during the afternoon. Joe and I fished that morning hitting all of the places we had caught fish the previous days and continued looking for more productive areas. As noon approached, we spotted Jeff moving into the area where Joe and I were fishing and, within a few moments, we were discussing the morning's catch. At that time, we decided to eat our lunches.

Now before I get into the next part of this story, let me give you a little background. Joe and I were fishing out of his boat which is a Bass Tracker, a nice boat he bought several years ago at a bargain. He keeps it looking really nice and tries to maintain it — unlike me. I use the heck out of mine and have been accused of abusing it. However, my thinking is that it is a boat used for fishing. If I need to get to an area where the fish are, then the boat is going there. Now the day before, Joe, in his never-ending inspection of the boat, noticed one of the screws holding the front pedestal seat to the boat had backed itself out a little; therefore, he promptly tightened it. What he neglected to notice was the wood had rotted.

As we were sitting there talking, Jeff was fixing our lunch of bologna--a good half-inch thick-- with tomato, cheese, and mustard between two slices of bread; potato chips; a can of pork n beans; and a good, cold soda. (Now that's a fisherman's dream lunch!) I was telling the story of Joe falling out of the boat into Mallard Lake, a lake outside of Blytheville where he and I fished for years together. Joe had caught a really nice crappie weighing over two pounds and it got hung up in the brush. While he was leaning over to free the fish, Joe toppled over the side. The last thing he uttered before he hit the water was "Help!" When someone starts falling, there is nothing you can do to help them so you just as well laugh and that is just what I did. Now I have heard what comes around goes around. Some say it is "karma." I don't know what to blame it on but I do know this: I had no more than gotten this out of my mouth and Jeff said, "Here is your sandwich." As I turned and leaned back to reach for it, it happened. Head over heels into the lake I went! I'm always amazed how fast events can change. A moment before I was sitting dry in a boat laughing at the story of Joe, but now I'm standing in water up to my chest, wet from head to toe with a soggy sandwich in my hand, asking for help to get back into the boat, and hearing nothing but laughter coming from Joe and Jeff. After a few minutes, they wiped the tears of laughter out of their eyes and managed to get me back into the boat. As usual when I get into these fixes, I do it with an audience. While I was getting my wet, muddy shoes off and removing my socks and shirt, another fisherman came by and asked me if the water was cold. He also recommended that I not swim in this area because the day before he saw three alligators in the same spot. According to him, one of them was over six feet long. As it turned out while fishing in the same area the next day we got pictures of four alligators within thirty yards of where I'd fallen in the day before. I'm sure if I had known that, I could have jumped back into the boat without Joe's and Jeff's help!

All things considered, the trip went OK because we caught some really nice fish, my shoes and clothes dried so that I was able to wear them again, and I didn't get eaten by gators. The worst thing about it: there wasn't any more bologna.

Thanks Joe and Jeff for the memories.

MY DAYS OF PLAYING TARZAN

By: Jim Ferguson

In response to one of my stories, "Cowboys and Stick Horses," my sister Sandy reminded me of the days we lived in Mississippi and suggested I write a story of the times we played Tarzan--an era of my life I had forgotten. We moved to Mississippi while I was in the fourth grade at the age ten. (Now I know some of you are probably thinking by the time I was in the fourth grade I had to be at least thirteen or fourteen but I wasn't.) "Tarzan" was the big hit at that time in the movie theaters across America. The first stories of Tarzan were written by Edgar Rice Burroughs in 1911; the first film of "Tarzan of the Apes" debuted on January 27, 1918 and was first filmed in Morgan City, Louisiana and was a silent movie. Some of the actors playing Tarzan during the silent movie era were Gene Pollar, a New York fireman; P. Dempsey Tabler, an opera singer; Jim Pierce, a foot ball player; and Frank Merrill, a gymnast. Frank Merrill was the first actor to put a voice to Tarzan. However the most famous Tarzan was Johnny Weissmuller who played the role in "Tarzan the Ape Man" which filmed by MGM and also starred Maureen O'Sullivan as Jane.

For the first time in my life I lived in a town: Rosedale, Mississippi. It was a small southern town with a couple of small factories and many beautiful, old plantation-style homes. Built by cotton farmers, some of these homes were over a hundred years old. Once again, cotton was king and the main means of making a living. Just as he did in Missouri, Dad farmed and we spent a lot of hours in the fields chopping and picking cotton. But on the days that we were not in the cotton fields, I continued searching for adventures and this small southern town was full of them for a country boy! Moving into a new town and starting to a new school is never easy. You always have to find your place and there is always someone who wants to challenge your right to belong and to mix with the local kids. With a few discussions after school in the alleys and giving/receiving black eyes and bloody noses, I found my place within the pecking order and made friends. Life went on and I continued to seek new adventures. One of the advantages of living in town was we were able to go to the movies. At this time, the best movies showing were ones of Tarzan. This small Mississippi town was made for kids who watched them and then pretended to be Tarzan. One part of the block where we lived was a cane thicket. Now I'm not talking about the small cane we have here in southeast Missouri. Rather this was bamboo twenty feet high and as big around as a can of pork and beans at the base. The new friends and I built bamboo huts in that area which was an absolutely perfect place to pretend to be a jungle. In addition to the bamboo, there were also wisteria vines growing on the trees which were excellent for cutting and swinging from tree to tree which indeed, made this a perfect place for me and my new friends to meet and play. My new friends were Guy Whitney, David

Moore (his dad was the local doctor), Wally Wilson, Lee (who was Wally's sister and was nicknamed "Lee Baby"). Lee was a real tomboy. Another friend was Thumper. Over the years I have forgotten his real name but, hey, that was forty-nine years ago. We just always called him Thumper. I do recall he had a sister who was in the Miss Mississippi Pageant. She sure was a pretty girl. On Saturday mornings we would step out into our respective yards and let loose with our "Tarzan calls" and await the answering calls from each other. Then we met in our jungle and began playing Tarzan. Another place we enjoyed playing was across the levy. Since Rosedale was built on the Mississippi River, the levy ran along the edge of town. There were a lot of woods between the levy and the river. The older boys who had climbed those trees before us had cut enough wisteria vines that we could actually swing from one tree to the next and then grab another vine and keep swinging as many as five or six times--a true Tarzan paradise. We had a lot of fun and made a lot of memories there. One of the best parts it that I don't ever recall anyone ever getting seriously hurt. On the opposite side of the levy these older boys had dug tunnels where we could go into one tunnel and crawl several feet before popping up in another hole—just like a bunch of prairie dogs. This was also a good place for dirt clod fights. My first unsupervised camping trip was on that levy. Thumper and I took our sleeping bags, a couple of eggs apiece, and a skillet and spent the night there under the southern Mississippi stars. Once again, something for which parents today would be charged with child neglect for allowing their kids to do this.

And as always, time passes and changes all things. We only lived in Rosedale one year and then returned to live in Gideon, the small town in southeast Missouri where time continued to pass and I grew up. However a few years ago I made a road trip to Lake Village, Arkansas, to fish and visit with some old friends. On my way home I paid a visit to the small town of Rosedale, Mississippi and was amazed at how the town had changed. Both the factories had closed but the theater was still there but was all boarded up. The beautiful old homes looked as though they had been neglected and the house where we lived was no longer there. The worst part was the bamboo forest where we played Tarzan wasn't there. In its place were two or three trailer houses. The woods on the other side of the levy were gone and cotton fields had been planted. I did manage to find one of my friends, David Moore. During our visit he told me his dad died a year or so after we moved. He continued that he had neither seen nor heard from Thumper in twenty years but Wally Wilson played pro golf for a while and was now a golf pro at a country club in Jackson, Mississippi. Wally's sister, Lee, who had never married and was still very much a tomboy, was a successful business lady in Alabama or Georgia. As for Guy, he went to Viet Nam, came home, and never was the same and just drifted away. While sitting on the porch with David, I asked if he could still give the Tarzan yell. He laughed. We both gave it a try and affirmed that time <u>does</u> change all things.

Thanks, Sandy, for renewing these memories!

ME AND DAN

By: Terry Weldon

Growing up in a family of ten Aunts and Uncle, I had lots of cousins and I was very close to all of them. Each relationship was different. Danny Beasley was one that was like a brother. We spent most weekends together either at their house or ours. One weekend Danny was spending the night with me and we had made us a campfire in the back yard near the smoke house. We were sharper than most boys our age and we had, earlier that day, soaked several corncobs in a pan of gasoline to help them burn better in the campfire, (you can already see we were pretty sharp!). Thinking like a true boy scout, I had placed the pan just under the edge of the smokehouse to keep it away from the fire. As Danny and I sat by the fire talking about the week's events and what we were going to do after we were done being astronauts, he would place the tip of a long stick he had in the gasoline and them light it over the fire. I'm pretty sure he was chasing bugs with the flame on the tip of the stick. After a stream of gasoline had built up between the pan and the fire, it finally lit, running straight to the pan of gas, and up it went, setting just under the edge of the smokehouse. Being afraid it would burn the smokehouse down, I grab the handle of the pan and attempted to toss it over the garden fence where it would do no damage. The handle on the old pan was hallow and worn, causing the pan to spin upside down and pour the gasoline all over my me from the waist down. In an instant I was a ball of fire. Danny took off running into the house, while I decided to head for the road ditch which was full from the rain we had earlier that day. We were in the back yard and the ditch was in front of our house, so, as I began to run, the flames got even higher. Knowing pretty quickly this wasn't going to work, I looked for some other way to put out the fire, I spotted the water faucet at the edge of the back porch and decided to get under it and turn on the water, as I squatted and turned on the water, Danny came running out of the house with a blanket from the bed. He jumped me like a flea on a hound dog. For a moment I am sure we looked like a midget wrestling team rolling all over the back yard. After the fire was out he told me he had learned in cub scouts earlier that week to wrap the victim in a blanket and that is what he was going to do. I was burned pretty bad on both legs and missed working in the fields that summer, which didn't break my heart, however I also missed playing baseball that summer and that did upset me. Looking back, I've often wondered how bad I would have gotten burned, if Dan hadn't rolled me up in the blanket.

Danny and I use to do a lot of rabbit hunting also. His dad, Uncle Ed, tried his best to teach us how to find a rabbit setting and shoot it with a slingshot. We got pretty good with the slingshots, but we never could spot the rabbit setting to shoot it. Uncle Ed would complain about how many bullets we fired and how few rabbits we brought home. One very cold winter day just outside of Campbell Missouri, Danny and I were hunting when we came across a stack of irrigation pipe. We were checking the grass all around the stack of pipes, when we scared up a rabbit and we saw it run into one of the pipe. It was one of the pipe on the bottom of the stack, so, Danny layed down and fired his 22 rifle into the pipe killing the rabbit. Now, that would have been genius, except, now we couldn't get the rabbit out of the pipe. The pipe being on the bottom of the stack, we began unstacking them to get to the one with the rabbit in it. As we got down to the last three levels of pipe, we discovered another rabbit inside. This time I turned the pipe up on one end and the rabbit slid right down into Danny's hands. We were getting really excited now. One pipe had two rabbits in it. That day we took 6 rabbits home and fired one bullet. Uncle Ed enjoyed our story and was happy we had saved our bullets, however, he wasn't too happy to hear we shot a hole in the farmer's irrigation pipe!

Danny and I lived in different counties and we never had the chance to play baseball against each other until our senior year. It was going to be the game of the century. The entire family was going to be there to see us battle. I was a pitcher with a mean curve ball and Dan was a lead off batter, that always hit the first ball. We had teased each other for several weeks about how bad we were going to beat each other. Unfortunately, just before the game was to be played, I went to Florida on our Senior trip and was unable to play against Danny. I know he has always wondered about that game, but, I am sure I would have struck him out...

THE JOURNEY

By: Jim Ferguson

My name is Isaiah Sexton and I was born in 1793 in a settlement deep in the hills of the Clinch Mountains of Tennessee. I am now 56 years of age. I am holed up in a cave in the Rocky Mountains because I'm injured. I have been here three days now and I'm feeling myself getting weaker with each passing day. There is water flowing from a spring in the rear of this cave, and I also have fire and food. I feel that I am coming to the end of a long journey as I have been coughing up blood since my horse and I fell three days ago. I am sure I busted something loose on the inside. I started this journey almost forty years ago.

I left my home in the Clinch Mountains in a hurry after being involved in a fight with another young man over a woman. Fearing that I killed him, I returned to my home and grabbed the old flintlock rifle off the mantel along with some powder and shot and placed them in my possible bag. I then quickly grabbed some jerky, my only other pair of clothes, and headed out into the night. As I made my way through the woods that night, setting some distance between me and the settlement, I began formulating an idea as to where I would go--with little knowledge as to what lay west of my home. I had heard from others in the settlement who had traveled west that there is a river about five days southwest of here that heads west. I knew that would be the direction I would go because the west was opening up and a man could lose himself there. And at the moment that was what I needed to do.

The father of the boy I killed was very rich and I knew I would have to get far away fast and never return home again.

Stopping only for a quick nap or two, I made it to the river in four days. With gathered driftwood I built a small raft that I could use to make the journey down river. Then I built a small fire to cook a possum I had killed that morning. Although I'm not fond of eating possum I could hardly wait until it was done because my backbone was wearing a hole into the front of my shirt from hunger. After eating my fill I stretched out and managed to get a few hours sleep.

Around midnight I began the second leg of my journey by shoving the raft into the water and heading south by southwest on the Tennessee River. I knew it would be a long float but, without a horse, there was no other choice and was the best I could do. With the spring rains still running out of the creeks, the river had a good flow. I was able to put several miles between my past and me. I have been on the river for five days now. As the sun was beginning to set, I rounded a bend in the river and saw some bluffs which would make a good place to spend the night. The bluffs would offer shelter from the storm that seemed to be brewing in the western sky. Pulling ashore I began walking along the bluff and gathering driftwood for the night's fire when I noticed carved into the rock the initials "SK"--those same initials I had seen before carved into rocks and trees around my Clinch Mountain home. The story is told they are the initials of a man who lived far back in the Clinch Mountains years ago and was one of the first to settle there. The story says he was a "long hunter" who would leave his home for extended periods of time searching new places. It was also said he left his "sign" far and wide and could even be found in the far western lands extending all the way to the great Rocky Mountains.

I awoke the next morning to find the storm that had rolled in around midnight still raging. The river had risen several feet and was threatening my camp. I also discovered my raft had drifted away. Being afraid of the rising water I braved the storm in search of better shelter and additional firewood. I was able to find better shelter in the form of a cave just a short distance from the bluff. Returning to my camp I retrieved my belongings and a torch from the fire. At the cave, I placed the torch in a small fire pit and added more wood. The cave soon came to life. I gave thanks to "SK" for marking this spot on the river for me. It was truly a blessing.

With the fire now roaring I again took a piece of wood from it and used it as a torch to look around the cave. I was amazed at what I discovered close to the rear of the cave. Lying on its side was a dugout canoe and, by the amount of dust that had settled on it, I would say it had been there a long time. It seemed to be as solid as the day it was made. As I moved the canoe to its upright position I noticed something else behind it. Against the wall were four flat rocks stacked. Having used stacking rocks myself as a young man to leave signs, I began to search around. Below the rocks buried a few inches in the floor of the cave there were four gold coins. Gauging their appearance I took them to be Spanish coins. For the first time since leaving my home I felt a sense of relief! I now had a good canoe and money in my pocket; maybe things would work out. With the rain still coming down and the river rising, I spent the biggest part of the next six days in the shelter of the cave venturing out only to hunt for food. I made jerky from the game I was able to kill. I still had a long way to go on the river and would need the food.

On the seventh day I decided it was time for me to continue on my journey down the Tennessee River. It would take several weeks to arrive at the Ohio River and then another several days to reach the point where the Ohio dumped into the Mississippi. As I loaded my things into the canoe and before shoving off, I took the time to carve initials into the bluff below those of "SK." Fearing the danger of leaving a true sign of my passing, I carved the initials "JW" and took on the name of "James Wesley." I left that cave with a new name and a new life.

The Tennessee River flows south for several hundred miles before turning back north and emptying into the Ohio. As a result I had been on the river for weeks but at last I reached the Ohio River. After a few more days I would turn south once again on the Mississippi River. Considering the distance I had traveled, it was an uneventful trip. I saw several Indian tribes camped along the river but all were peaceful Cherokees who only waved as I went by their camps. After a few more days on the river I approached the mouth of the Ohio. Looking across the Mississippi I was amazed at the size of it. Never in my life have I seen such a huge river! It was well into the summer now and the river is low, but the amount of water was still breathtaking. As nervous as I was, I pointed the canoe downstream and headed south working my way to the westward bank. Traveling another three days I pulled ashore at the small settlement of New Madrid.

As I ascended the banks of the river and entered the town I felt a great uneasiness about me — a feeling I have often had when bad things were about to happen. Ma always told me that I had the gift of foresight. However the relief of being with civilization again soon overtook the dark mood. After spending several days in New Madrid and not wanting to leave the company of people, I decided I would stay in this logging town for a while. I set myself to the task of finding a job and a place to stay. Finding a job with one of the loggers was easy. I found a place to live that had wood sides, a canvas tarp for the roof, and a dirt floor. As the days and weeks passed, summer and fall came and went. The work was hard but the pay was fair and I managed to sock some back. When December approached the weather became cold and, along with it, the uneasiness returned that I had felt the first day I landed on the shore and walked into town. For some reason, it wouldn't go away this time but, rather, worsened with each passing day.

On December 16, 1811 at 2 a.m., I knew the reason for my fear. I was awakened by the sound of a large boom followed by the shaking of the earth. It felt as if the ground had dropped out from under me. Making my way outside of the tent I noticed the town was in great panic. Trees were falling, houses were collapsing, and even the river banks were falling off into the river. The river itself seemed to be rising and falling with waves as big as one would see on the ocean. Some people were running, screaming, and crying while others were on their knees praying. During the course of the next several days the earthquakes continued. Stories were being told of fissures erupting and spewing sand and sulfur into the air. News came in of the land itself sinking several feet and forming large sink holes and small lakes. There were even stories of the Mississippi River flowing backwards forming a large lake on the Tennessee side of the river and killing a large Indian population that lived there! All of this caused the traveling Bible-thumpers to declare that the pits of hell had opened up and they were calling for all to repent in order to save themselves from an eternity in hell and damnation. As the weeks and months continued to pass, the earthquakes continued.

Deciding it was time for me to take my leave, I loaded my dugout with my belongings which included some things I had bought for trading purposes and once again pointed it south. This time I had only to travel a few miles until I would come to a portage where it was said I could head west by going through the swamps for several miles until I reached a sand ridge, cross over it, then travel northwest on the St. Francis River. Crossing the swamps was a little more than I expected it to be because there were cypress trees as big as three and four feet through, snakes and frogs bigger than any I had ever seen, and mosquitoes big enough to suck all your blood out in one bite it seemed. Having lived in the Clinch Mountains all my life I had never seen anything like it. After spending a few nights on earthen mounds built by Indians in the past I finally made it to the sand ridge I was told about. Building a travois for my dugout I forded it across the sand ridge to the backwater of the St Francis River in just three days. Yet it was a long, hard three days.

Upon launching my dugout I found the river to be small--nothing like the Tennessee, Ohio, or the Mississippi but instead a slow, lazy river winding through more swamps. It was easy paddling until I reached the hill where it became a little more swift thereby slowing my progress. Upon reaching the hill part of the river, I came upon a tribe of Wappapello Indians who had lived along the river for years. Peaceful they were. I was able to trade some of the things I had bought in New Madrid for a well-made bow and some arrows which I knew would come in handy since I was already running low on lead for the old flintlock I had with me. They told me of a white man's settlement a few more miles upriver that was no more than two days just past the point where the two big springs empty into the river. The remaining trip to the white settlement of Greenville was an enjoyable trip. I found the hills to be smaller than those of the Clinch Mountains.

Upon arriving at the settlement I was greeted by a man named Marler. As we talked he told me the river would be too low to travel in my dugout and if I was planning on going further west I would need a horse. After spending a few days in Greenville I once again began thinking about what I was going to do and where was I heading. Now that I was several hundred miles away from my past I wasn't too concerned about being found. However this journey I began as a means of escaping was beginning to take on a new purpose. I was young and had enjoyed seeing the lands that I had traveled through and was desirous to see more of this country. After making a trade of my dugout for supplies and purchasing a horse and saddle I said my goodbyes to Marler and the others I had met in Greenville and headed southwest to a place known as the Texas Territory.

It was now late in the summer of 1812 and I was hoping I could make it to Texas before winter set in. Traveling along the hills and staying east of the Indian nation I worked my way southwest. Only on occasion did I meet any settlers or travelers which made the trip lonely, but by this time I had become accustomed to it. The lay of the land changed very little until two months later when I reached the Texas Territory. The hills then faded, the land flattened, and the vegetation became more scrubby and arid looking. After three months of travel I reached the Texas town of Nacogdoches-- known by many at that time as being the gateway to the Texas frontier. Most of its residents were of Spanish descent. However there were a few Americans beginning to settle there. Since it was hard for me to communicate with local residents, it took a while to find a place to stay or work. But within a week (with the help of another American I met) a Mexican ranch owner agreed to give me a chance to become a vaquero. Over the course of the next few months I adapted to the work and became quite skilled at roping the horses. I seemed to have a knack for working with them. The work was hard but I soon learned the language and enjoyed the culture of the Spanish people. A new life I was seeking and a new life I had found. My days in Texas soon turned into months and the months soon turned into years. I had now been there for ten years and managed to melt into the Spanish culture and was completely accepted by the people. I had worked, caught, broke, and trained thousands of horses during those ten years as well as made several drives into Mexico to sell them. The day I celebrated my greatest achievement was the day I married Maria, the daughter of a Spanish ranch owner. Those few months were the happiest of my life. After having been married to Maria for two years, the past had faded and seemed more of a dream; yet, there seemed to be something dogging me. It was the same feeling I once had upon entering the town of New Madrid--uneasiness that something wasn't right. I was not able to figure it out. Life was great and Maria and I were happy. In fact, we were more than happy the day she told me that I was to be a dad. The baby was expected to arrive in July. That gave me six months--plenty of time to add a room onto our adobe house and to build a cradle for our child.

While roping a young colt in late afternoon one hot summer day, I noticed a trail of dust rising off in the distance. As the dust swirled closer I could tell it was a rider and wondered what fool would be running a horse that fast and that far in this sweltering summer heat. As he approached I could hear him shouting my name. When the vaquero slid to a halt beside me, he told me I was needed back at the hacienda and that I should not spare the horse getting there. Leaping from my horse I busted into the room only to be met by my mother-in-law and father-in-law with tears streaming down their cheeks. They informed me that my Maria and our baby died during childbirth. On July 21, 1824, with a heavy heart, I threw the last spade of dirt over my wife and child. I blamed myself for this: it must have been my punishment for taking a life back in Tennessee. Wiping the tears from my eyes I climbed onto my horse and rode away. I vowed that never again would someone else have to pay for my sins.

I left Texas with a broken heart. With no purpose in life I aimlessly traveled the southwest for the next ten years living among the Spanish people and working as a ranch hand from time to time. I also lived with various Indian tribes in the Sierra Madre Mountains in Central Mexico where I witnessed the migration of hundreds of thousands of butterflies to that area. This gave me a new purpose in life. If I could not enjoy the beauty of my Maria, then I would learn to seek out and enjoy the beauty this country had to offer.

Leaving Mexico I began traveling north toward the Rocky Mountains following the Rio Colorado northward. I found myself engulfed in a large canyon unlike anything I had ever seen. It was as if the Rio Colorado River had sliced the earth in half: giant bluff, raging rapids, but yet a peacefulness and beauty like no other. The weeks and months I spent traveling in and around the canyon were appealing but encountering no one other than a few Indian tribes encamped along the river began to weigh heavy. Once again pointing my horse toward the north, I continued further into the Rocky Mountains.

One cool, summer morning of 1836 I met up with a man by the name of Jim Bridger who was exploring the Rockies for a passage west. I gained huge amounts of information from him about the Rockies. He told me of the travel of others and their findings. He mentioned a man by the name of Joe Meeks, a mountain man who spent time trapping and exploring the Rockies by traveling along the Yellowstone. He described it as a giant cauldron where steam and the smell of sulfur spewed forth from the earth with hot pools of water and geysers. It was a very inhospitable place to be. In fact, the coming winter would make it almost unlivable. After spending several days with Bridger, I was able to buy a pack horse and some trapping supplies from him by using one of the gold coins I had found several years ago in a cave along the Tennessee River. I took my leave from him and headed north following the Big Piney River to the Big Horn River with only a short time left before the winter snow would began to fall.

I searched out a good place to spend the winter and constructed a place for me to stay through the coming winter, stock piling wood for fuel, killing game and making as much jerky as I could. I also gathered as many acorns and other nuts as possible. Since beaver was plentiful, I soon had trapped a plentiful supply resulting in several hides that I was able to tan and sew into winter clothing and moccasins. Tending to my horses was my biggest problem. Building them a shelter connected to mine was the easy part, but providing them with enough winter feed was problematic. I collected as much of the wild grasses from along the river as I could binding them with pieces of rawhide I made from the beaver pelts and stored them inside the shelters.

While I was running my traps one morning during the middle of September, I noticed a rider following the river. As he approached he hailed me, dismounted from his horse, and introduced himself as Charles Lipton. Turns out, he was a trapper who was camped further on up the Big Horn and was keeping company with several other trappers who had been trapping the Big Horn for several years. They first came here with the American Fur Company with William Sublett and Robert Cambell. He shared with me that I could go with them to the fur company when spring came to sell my furs and do some trading. Realizing that I was a greenhorn he suggested that I travel back with him to withstand the winter. Considering all the work I had done the last few weeks I declined. Upon hearing this, Charles stayed on with me for a few more days helping me gather more grass and feed for my horse. We also took an overnight trip to a valley where we killed a buffalo--my first. Although I had heard of them, I was still amazed at the size and the amount of meat on them. This would be plenty to last me through the winter plus the hide would make good winter clothing. As the dawn broke on the seventh day of his visit, the gray clouds began to roll in. Taking notice of the approaching winter, he gathered his things, mounted his horse, and wished me luck with hopes of seeing me next spring for the rendezvous. He pointed his horse back upriver toward his camp.

Two days after his departure I awoke with the first snow of the season on the ground and was hit with the realization that the time of gathering nuts and roots for the winter was over. I certainly hoped I had enough to last me. I then set myself to the task of setting more beaver traps and seeing that my horses ate as much of the grasses as they could before the snow became too deep for them to feed. As the days and weeks passed the snow got deeper. Building myself a pair of snowshoes using willows from the river and strips of beaver hide allowed me to continue to set and run my traps. Taking the time and effort to bust the ice off the ponds resulted in an increased workload along with a decrease in the number of beavers being trapped.

By mid-December the snow was several feet deep and the beaver ponds were covered with a foot of ice. There was nothing for the horses to feed on other than what I had stored for them. My days were filled with the stretching and tanning of the hides I had trapped. The best to my figuring on Christmas morning I awoke to the sound of a single bull buffalo blowing outside my cabin. What he was doing here alone I have no idea but needing and wanting the fresh meat, I shot him and butchered him and packed him in the snow outside my cabin. Carrying the hide inside I spent the next several day tanning it and then placed it against the wall to help keep the cold winter air outside. As the new year rolled in, the snow continued to fall. Having never wintered in the Rockies before I was beginning to think that by spring the snow would have me buried. The cold continued as more months passed. The deep silence was broken only by the howling of the wind and the sounds of the horses.

As May approached, the number of days the sun shone increased. Hoping for an early thaw I prepared my hides for hauling. Taking advantage of the warmer days I ventured out of the cabin to gather firewood by breaking some limbs from the small trees. The first sounds of spring came by way of snow melting and dripping from the eves of the cabin. Soon small patches of ground could be seen and the horses chomped on the small blades of grass as soon as they appeared.

By the end of May I built a travois for the packhorse, saddled up, and began the trip upriver hoping to arrive at the camp where Charles Lipton spent the winter. I planned to join the group for the journey to the rendezvous. Coming into their camp only in time to see them leaving, I caught up with Charles who was quite surprised to see me and happily introduced me to the other members of his party. It felt great to be in the company of others as we traveled the next few days on our way to Fort Union where we would sell our furs. The rendezvous seemed to be the gathering place for the mountain men many of whom had weathered the winter alone in the mountains just as I had done. It was a joyous time for all and included quite a bit of drinking. Gambling and fighting took place along with the trading of supplies and the telling of stories of the past winter. New places were discussed but the Yellowstone was one of the most interesting I heard mentioned. After spending two weeks at the rendezvous I said my good-byes, packed my supplies, and started the journey to the Yellowstone.

It took several days but at last I reached the area known as Yellowstone. And if there is a more beautiful place on earth, then God has hidden it from man. The tall pines that reached the clouds and the beautiful valleys where deer, elk, and moose fed were thrilling. I witnessed my first huge herd of buffalo and there are more of these big, strong animals than I can count. From the signs I have noticed it appears the streams are still full of beavers. It would be a good place to stay and trap but, after this past winter, I plan on being at a lower elevation come the next winter. First I am going to see all of this area I can. The last few weeks I have observed some rather unusual sights. I found bubbling pools of hot steaming water and geysers spewing hot water skyward for several feet. The smell of sulfur took away my breath at times. Although this area has its beauty there is also uneasiness about it as though at some time in history something really bad has happened here or it could possibly happen in the future. It's not as strong as the feeling I had when I entered New Madrid but it is more devastating and was too much for me to ponder at that time. It was time I should be heading to the lower country to start making preparations for the winter which comes early in the Rockies.

Putting the Yellowstone and its beauty behind me, I made my way toward the Mussel Shell which is also known to be beautiful and full of beavers. While fording several rivers I saw some of the biggest waterfalls I had ever seen. The sound of the water cascading down was deafening at times but awesome to behold! Upon reaching the Mussel Shell I settled into a small cave in the back of a boxed canyon which would offer protection from the cold winter that would arrive shortly. By cutting a few logs and dragging them to the opening of the cave I was able to reduce the entrance size thereby making it easier to heat. With the preparation of my new home completed I began the chores of cutting firewood, gathering and storing feed for the horses, and setting my beaver traps. Acorns, hickory nuts, and walnuts were plentiful and would make good eating come winter. By the first snowfall I was ready. And as always, time passes. Days and weeks turned into months. When spring rolled around, I attended a rendezvous and sold my furs while enjoying the company of the other mountain men. I was also engaged in some trading. Although the two horses I had were beginning to get some age on them, I was able to make a trade with one of the other traders. In exchange for the horses, I received a young mare horse and a mule. Since the mule was stronger than the horse it made a better pack animal.

Leaving the rendezvous I returned to the Mussel Shell. Since I did not have to worry about finding shelter for the coming winter I took advantage of the time and made several two-to-three day trips looking around and doing a little prospecting. There was no gold to be found in these hills. I met and did some trading with a Crow party on one trip and a Blackfoot party on the other and found them to be of a friendly sort in spite of my having heard stories of raids they have committed on others moving in or traveling through the area.

During the course of the next four years I was able to catch and sell hundreds of beaver and other furs. Not having the desire for strong drink nor the weakness of gambling enabled me to put aside a good amount of money. Since my age was beginning to make itself known by this time, I loaded my mule and saddled my horse in the spring of 1843. Leaving my mark "JW" carved on the cave wall, I pointed my horse to the western sky and left the Mussel Shell.

At the last rendezvous I learned the price for beaver was falling. It seemed the desire to have beaver skin hats had faded at home and abroad. I also learned the west was opening up. James Sinclair and others are bringing people west by the wagonloads to "Ouragon" (Oregon). Cattle and sheep have been driven north to Portland and there is talk about it becoming a territory. It is the fear of a lot of the mountain men that their days of roaming the Rockies and trapping are numbered. As for me, my age alone is taking care of that and the winters are getting harder on me as is the loneliness of the long winter.

As I traveled westward I passed through the Big Hole and the Bitterroot River Basins. I had heard the Bitterroot River was a good beaver place a few years ago. I also passed through the Cascade Mountain Range and met the tribe members of the Nez Perce and the Chinook Indians before I reached my destination of the meeting place of the Snake and Columbia Rivers. Upon reaching this point and with the need to let my horse and mule rest a few days, I began the search for a good meadow with tall grass and good water for them. After unpacking the mule and unsaddling the horse I picketed them out and began looking for some type of shelter nearby. Once again I was quite fortunate to find shelter under an overhanging cliff with a natural nook set back ten feet or so within the hillside. As is often the case when locating a natural camping place like this, there was a fire pit already in place. No doubt it had been used several times by traveling hunting parties throughout history. After gathering dry driftwood along the creek where the animals were picketed I built a small fire. I then grabbed my rifle and went to hunt for some fresh meat. Spotting a large boar coon perched in the fork of a persimmon tree I shot him out, cleaned him, and took him back to the camp and put him to roasting for the night's meal. As the sun began to set in the valley I moved the animals closer to the camp, gathered up my bed roll, and settled in for the night.

As I lay there listening to the night sounds and watching the firelight flicker up on the rock wall of the small cave, I noticed something I hadn't seen since leaving Tennessee. Carved into the wall next to my head were the initials "SK." I did not get much sleep that night although I was very tired. Seeing those initials set me to pondering about all the years that had passed from the time I first saw them carved along the banks of the Tennessee River. I have traveled to Texas, down into Mexico, and back up through the Rockies. I have grown old since leaving my home. I am constantly fighting the urge to load up some day and return. Thirty-two years have passed since then. I am fifty years old and it was definitely time to settle down in some place where the winters weren't so cold and the living conditions were better. I'm sure my maw and paw have both passed on. My young brothers and sisters would be grown with grown kids of their own. Here I lay with no family of my own and no specific place to call home--just a few coins in my pocket, a mule, a horse, and rambling feet. I knew the reason why I left home: being afraid to face up to what I had done. But I wondered why SK went away. I speculated as to how many times he returned to the Clinch Mountains during his lifetime. Was the reason for his wandering the thrill of adventure or seeing what was over the next mountain or across the next river? If so then I could partially understand it because I, too, have enjoyed the wandering and seeing things I would have never seen otherwise. But I have also missed home!

On my fourth day in the valley a cool wind blew in reminding me that fall had arrived and I still had a long way to go yet before reaching Portland. I loaded the mule and saddled up and left the valley. Of course before leaving I, too, carved my initials "JW" below those of SK. As the days passed I worked my way around the Columbian Gorge and saw some petroglyphs on a cliff wall. From their appearance they seemed to have been there for many years, if not centuries, which reminded me that even though this is considered a new world people have been living here for hundreds, perhaps even thousands, of years. During the course of the next several days of working my way to Portland I crossed the Columbian Gorge, and The Dalles, while following the Columbia River until I finally reached the settlement of Portland.

Finding a place to settle in for the winter wasn't much of a problem once I met a couple of men by the names of William Overton and Asa Lovejoy. They were partners who owned Portland and were trying hard to develop it by bringing people in from across the country via the new Oregon Trail. With winter approaching and some money in my pocket, I declined looking for work. However by the spring of 1844 I was tired of not having anything to do so I took a job with Kit Carson bringing people into Oregon and California. Although I had much experience in traveling a big part of the so-called Oregon Trail while trapping beaver the last twenty years, this job still had its problems trying to get the heavy wagons across the mountain passes. One of the difficulties involved dealing with some of the greenhorns from back east who had their hearts set on finding riches in the western territory. After spending the next two years (1845 and 1846) in the Portland area, I decided the rainy weather wasn't to my liking. In addition I had not seen the Pacific Ocean as of yet. These two facts spurred me to once again throw the saddle on my old horse, buy supplies, and pack them onto an old mule I was able to purchase. Pointing them both south by southwest, I headed out for California.

As I wandered south I spent the biggest part of 1847 looking over the northern part of California and admiring the giant red wood trees. They were four to five times bigger than the ones we had back in my Clinch Mountains of Tennessee. They were two to three hundred feet high and as much as thirty feet around and often blocked the sun's rays from reaching the floor of the forest. They were one of the most spectacular things I had seen in all my years of roaming the western frontier. Now being from Tennessee I had never seen anything bigger than the Mississippi River. With that in mind you can guess how surprised I was when my eyes first fell upon the Pacific Ocean. The pounding of the waves against the shore was deafening and the smell of the salt water soon filled my nostrils even though I really didn't care for it. It was still alluring. I have heard it said by those who have spent time at sea that once it gets into your blood you will forever want to return. As I gaze upon the vastness of the ocean I can see where the mystery of it could make one want to sail away in search of other lands and the excitement it could bring. However, for me, I have spent my life on solid ground and the mounting years have taken their toll on me so on solid ground I will stay. But I do wish that I had the experiences that a time at sea would have given me.

After spending several months along the coast enjoying the sites and wonders of northern California, I once again pointed my horse south and inland finding myself arriving at the small settlement of Coloma, California in the fall of 1847. Like most settlements, Coloma was situated next to a river--the South Fork American River. Upon making camp just outside of Coloma I settled in for the night. I spent the next couple of days riding around looking for someplace to make a more permanent camp and found just such a place up river of town. After a day or so of fixing up my camp I returned to Coloma where I met two men. James Marshall and John Sutter owned and operated a saw mill. In view of my advancing age I wasn't looking for a job in the timber business but work was something I was going to need. As luck would have it they told me they were looking for someone to hunt and supply meat for the loggers and the townspeople. The person who had been fulfilling this need had become ill and died a few days ago. As I wandered around the settlement I began to get an odd feeling about this place. This time that feeling wasn't like the previous feelings that I have gotten of impending danger but something different. Rather, it was a feeling as though something important would take place here.

Putting the notion aside I returned to my camp and began making preparations for the hunt. As the days and weeks passed I found myself enjoying the hunting and supplying of food for the workers at the mill. The game was plentiful and the weather ranged from cool to cold which meant I didn't have to worry so much about spoilage and enabled me to spend more time farther away from Coloma. I have always preferred to kill my meat some distance from where I was camped. This allowed me to save the game near my camp for the times when the bad weather made it harder to travel.

As the fall of 1847 passed and winter came on, I began to think once again of returning to my home — to my beloved Clinch Mountains. Surely enough time had passed that it would now be safe for me to return. Return to what I knew not. Were my brothers and sisters still alive? So much time has passed since I slipped out into the night so many years ago and started this journey. Returning home would be a whole new journey in itself. I'm over two thousand miles from home. A trip like that would be hard on me at the age of 55, but it is a journey I would love to make, to be able once again to look upon the Clinch Mountains where I was raised. I had decided that come spring I would once again saddle up my horse and pack mule and head out. This time I would not be aiming them toward the western sky but would be directing them to the sunrise in the east.

As December and the year of 1847 came to an end, January and 1848 started with me sitting at my camp dreaming and making plans for the spring. The days clicked by, *and as always, time passes and changes all things.* On January 24, 1848 while following the river looking for new timber to cut, John Sutter saw something shining in the river bed that would not only change my plans but would also change the whole country. Gold, yes, gold! By the spring and summer thousands of people would be flocking to this quiet, sleepy settlement of Coloma, California. All of them would be desperately looking for the shining gold found at Sutter's Mill. As the weeks passed and the rumor of John Sutter's discovery spread, more and more people flocked to Coloma. Claims were filed, fights erupted, prices for goods exploded. It seemed as though the ones who were going to get rich over this gold rush were the business owners. I, too, was making money as fast as I could kill game and bring it back to town. Not only was I able to sell big game such as deer but I was also able to sell anything from possums to coons to beavers and all for high prices.

In late June while on one of my hunting trips I found a large nugget of gold along a small creek. That discovery gave me the gold fever also. Spending the next two days panning in the small creek I was able to find enough gold to convince me to give up the hunting job and do more prospecting. If I could find twice this much then I would be able to leave here and head home with enough money to last me the rest of my life back in the Clinch Mountains. Not wanting to draw attention to myself by returning to Coloma, I remained there on my creek panning for gold from daylight until dark. I moved big rocks out of the creek and dug by hand until my fingers were raw and bloody. I continually reminded myself I wasn't here to get rich or become wealthy but rather to make just enough to allow me to return to my mountain home in Tennessee. By the time the end of July came, I had managed to fill three pokes of gold dust and nuggets.

Being satisfied with that amount I saddled my horse after taking time to stash my gold under an old stump and fervently hoping it would be there when I returned. I headed to Coloma to gather the mule and other supplies I would need for my journey home. Approaching Coloma I was amazed at the size to which it had grown since I was here only a short month ago. Tents were pitched and saloons and gambling halls had opened up. As I approached the mercantile store I heard gunfire coming from one of the gambling halls. Turning toward the shots I witnessed a man falling out the door and clenching his chest. Bright red blood began flowing out and down his shirt as he staggered and fell to the ground. As I stood there and watched, I heard someone say, "That is the last time Samuel Williamson will cheat at cards." Samuel Williamson--that name has been forever etched in my mind. As I looked down upon the dead man I knew it was the very same man because he was the exact spitting image of his father. Samuel Williamson, the dead man lying at my feet, is the same man I thought I had killed forty years ago and was the reason I left my Clinch Mountain home.

It's been three weeks now since I returned to my creek and gathered my gold and headed home. Until three days ago I was a happy man! I was headed home after forty years until my horse shied from the sound of a rattlesnake and we both fell. As he rolled over me I felt my chest being crushed and now I lie here knowing I haven't much time left. With my last ounce of strength I bury my three pokes of gold in the corner of the cave and place a flat rock upon them with the hope that someday someone will find them just as I found the gold coins along the Tennessee River many years ago. As I lay here fighting for one more breath, I am deeply saddened by the knowledge I will never make it back to my Clinch Mountain home. I gaze upon the wall where I have carved the initials "J.W." in addition to "Isaiah Sexton." I think I see...could it be...Maria, my darling, is that you?

THE PUMP HOUSE

By: Terry Weldon

We lived about a half mile outside of town; therefore, we didn't have "city" water. Instead we had a well in the back yard. Once the well was drilled, instead of a pump handle on top, we had an electric motor and pump. The pump had a small five or ten gallon tank on it so it wouldn't lose its prime I think. The problem with this configuration was it would freeze in the winter and burst the tank or the lines. To prevent this from happening, my Grandpa P.O. built a "pump house" around it. It was about four feet by four feet square and stood about three feet tall. In order to service the motor and pump, Grandpa put a removable roof over it and sort of sloped it so the rain would run off of it.

Our pump house sat out back under the tree about twenty five feet from the back porch. To keep this structure from being "unsightly" from the travelers going down the highway at seventy miles per hour, Grandpa put shingles on it to match the roof of our house. That would be ok, but he also shingled the sides to help insulate it from the cold weather. Inside the pump house was packed with insulation also keeping the cold out.

One summer night when I was about fourteen or fifteen years old, I had returned home from a evening out with my friends. It was a warm summer night so I raised my bedroom window next to my bed and lay with my head almost on the window seal enjoying the cool night air. As I was about to drift off to dreamland, my eyelids began to flicker. At first I thought it was lightening from a distant thunderstorm out of hearing range. I batted my eyes a couple of times to clear them and hoped I didn't have glaucoma at fifteen years of age. However, just before dosing off they began to flicker again. I opened them and stuck my head out the window, which was very easy, with no screen in it, to get a better look outside. The pump house was just out of my view until I turned and looked further into the back yard. To might surprise, the pump house was on fire and really starting to burn, but good! I jumped from my bed and ran to the front of the house where Granny and Grandpa slept, yelled out, "the pump house is burning, the pump house is burning"! My grandparents hit the floor running, Granny in her sleeping gown and me and Grandpa in our underwear, which I might add, mine looked a lot better than his, and we all headed out the back door to save the pump house. We all three stood there at first evaluating the situation, then Grandpa ran to the edge of the porch to grab the water hose and turn on the faucet, only to discover someone had cut the end of the water hose off for a siphoning hose, which is an entirely different story that we won't get into right now. Once he discovered there was no water available to put out the fire and the tar from the shingles was melting and beginning to drip down the back side of the pump house onto the tree trunk, which would start the tree burning and we would really be in trouble then. Grandpa yelled at me to grab the opposite side of the pump house roof and we could carry it away from the tree to a safer place. With a little reluctance in my voice I asked if we might not want to rethink that idea. In a somewhat different voice, he rephrased his request to where I understood perfectly, so I grabbed hold and we took off away from the tree. Because the tar from the shingles was melting and dripping from the roof, there were several balls of this hot tar across the yard back to the pump house, of which Grandpa stepped on most of them going back to fight the fire. Now here is where me and Forrest Gump had a few things in common, "stupid is as stupid does". When Grandpa's bare feet hit those little balls of hot tar, he began to do this strange dance, unlike anything I had ever saw him do before, actually I didn't know he could dance at all! Now back to me and Forrest Gump, I began to laugh, out loud. Yep, you heard me right, I laughed out loud at something not all of us gathered in the back yard that night thought was funny! I know Grandpa was in severe pain, but I thought I saw the tiniest of grins on my Granny's face that we never talked about, ever! As Grandpa sat on the back porch and peeled the tar balls and most of the skin off the bottom of his feet and the pump house burned to the ground, I thought boy this is going to make a funny story forty years from now!

THE BLUE HERON

By: Jim Ferguson

It is early — 3:45 a.m. and I need to get this coffee into the thermos so I can head out for opening day of duck season. I'm going with an older friend of mine. This morning should be another great experience.

Upon arriving at Harold's house, I see the front porch light is on as is the one in the kitchen, which means breakfast again. Harold's wife, Ruby, always has breakfast ready for us by the time I get here--

homemade biscuits, eggs, gravy, and bacon. Bless that sweet woman's heart! Why she does this is beyond me but much appreciated.

Upon entering the house I see Harold, as always, sitting there in his bib overalls one gallus still undone, giving himself his insulin shot, while Ruby is finishing up at the stove. Settling in Harold and I eat and drink our coffee with a little chitchat discussing the morning hunt. The weatherman mentioned a cold front would be pushing into the area later this evening. The cold should cause a new flight of ducks moving through ahead of the approaching storm.

After finishing breakfast, Harold put on the last of his clothing, grabbed his gun shells and coat, and headed for the truck for the short drive to the duck blind. After arriving at the blind Harold proceeded to step into the blind and get himself settled in for the morning hunt while I grabbed both bags of decoys and headed to the water to place them in the water to entice the first flock of ducks to drop in hopefully. In most cases both or all parties hunting would help with this chore but Harold doesn't get around so well any more and with the bank of the ditch being steep it is my job. Now Harold will provide instruction as to the way he wants them placed. After putting them out, we wait for first light and, hopefully, for some ducks to make their way down the ditch and over our decoys.

As we sat there and talked while waiting, I heard the squawk of a blue heron as it came flying up the ditch and over the decoys. Just as I was going to say something to Harold about it, the blue heron lit just above the decoys. Harold rose up and shot it. I grumbled at him and asked why he did that. Didn't he know that it would drift back downstream and get tangled up with the decoys and I would have to go remove it? His answer to me was, "Yep, I know that." He continued that when I got it to go ahead and bring it to the blind and he would teach me something.

After returning with the heron in tow, I pitched it at Harold's feet whereupon he proceeded to pluck the feathers from the breasts of the heron. Then he cut the two breasts out and wrapped them in a paper towel and informed me when the hunt was over he would show me what to do with it.

Around 10:30 we called it a morning, gathered the ducks we had killed, and headed back to Harold's house. Upon entering the house, Harold called for Ruby and asked her to fix us a sandwich out of the heron. Taking the heron Ruby washed it, sliced it up into thin slices, salted and peppered it, and rolled it in flour and fried it. Then she placed it between two slices of white bread with a little mustard and gave it to us for lunch. Now I want to say a word or two about Harold. He was from the old school. He grew up under hard conditions. During the depression, he hunted ducks commercially as a young boy; that is how his family made their living. They ate what they could capture, kill, or catch so this wasn't that unusual for him. However, I must say not ever having eaten heron before or after--I must admit that it was good. Therefore, the next time you hear of someone eating something that you wouldn't think edible, don't turn your nose up so quickly. Bon appetite!

In Memory of Harold Fielder.

THE GREAT AMERICAN WOMAN

By: Jim Ferguson

While talking to a friend of mine a few days ago the subject of our mothers came and how they lived, worked, and raised us especially under the condition of the times. This set me to wondering if the young women and mothers of today realize how much better they have it than their mothers and grandmothers. In order to give the woman of today a clue, let's go back in time to the late forties and fifties. Let's use my mother as an example. Being a woman and a mother who lived in a rural area, she would represent the woman of that era. She was married when she was sixteen at a time when large families were quite common. By the time she was twenty-five, she had four children and, by the time, she was thirty, she had six children. Now raising six children was a full-time job. Although "mothering" wasn't the only job she had, for now we will just stay with the raising of the children. This entailed ensuring the never-ending laundry of clothes, towels, bed sheets, etc. for her family of eight was always done. Laundering today only consists of taking the clothes out of a hamper, putting them in the washing machine, turning the knob and returning thirty to forty-five minutes later to put them in the dryer. Once again, this only requires turning a knob and returning in approximately an hour to hang them on a hanger or fold them and put them in a drawer. I have performed this task many times in my life, and it is easy. But let's look back to the early days. We will not go all the way back to the days of a scrub board but, rather, to the first days of washing machines. "Laundry day" was an all day affair-- often on Saturdays. The washer sat on the back porch and Mom either filled up the washer with cold water by means of a water hose cold or she heated water and filled the washer with a bucket. When the clothes were washed she ran them through the wringer to squeeze the soapy water out letting them fall into tubs filled with clean water. Then she would run them through the wringer once again to get as much water out of them as possible before she took them to the yard and hung them on a clothes line to dry. After getting the clean clothes hung on the line, she hoped and prayed it didn't rain or that a dust storm would not hit before she got them dried. We are not done with laundry yet. Remember the clothing of that time was not "wash and wear." The next chore in the rotation was the ironing of those clothes. So as you can see "laundry day" was just that--laundry day all day long. Now ask yourself if you would you like to go back to the "Good Old Days." Not me! Now let's not forget we have to feed these children. There were no microwave ovens and no fast food. Mom cooked and she cooked three meals a day. As for my mom, I don't remember a day in my life that when we got out of bed that she didn't have breakfast on the table or she was still cooking it. We never went to school without eating first. More often than not that included making home made biscuits. Today a lot of children don't eat breakfast until they get to school and how that ever got started I'm not sure, but it is the practice today. Let us not forget before Mom cooked these three meals, there were things to do and going to the store and buying them wasn't all there was to it. She planted a garden; she harvested that garden; and then she either froze or canned what had been harvested. Doing this also required a great deal of time out of her day and life was not an easy task. This task was often done at night alternating between canning and giving the children a bath, getting them ready for bed, and making sure that the school home work was done. "Good Old Days?" Now mothers have done the laundry and fed the children. While doing all of this they managed to clean the house, play doctor and stay up nights with sick ones, referee the fights, answer all the questions that the children threw at them while also finding time to make dresses and shirts for us out of the flour sacks. As if that weren't enough for our mothers to do they also worked in the fields or in town. Now as was the case for a lot of rural women, my mother worked in the fields often helping Dad with the planting of the crops. She always chopped the cotton in the summer and picked it in the fall and would leave the younger children at the house with one of the older ones. I have heard her tell the story that right after she and Dad married, they snapped cotton one winter trying to make some extra money. She said that is the coldest she has ever been in her life. My mother and millions like her across the U.S.A. did these things and were glad to do them for their family never asking for a lot. They would be so very proud of getting something as simple as a new rug for the living room floor and later crying as the north winds blew under the house and stretched and ruined it. Living in an old, drafty farm house meant having to sleep under several quilts to stay warm on cold winter nights. These quilts were very often made by them knowing that they had it better than their mothers before them. But as always time changes all things. Life is better today for the woman which is a great thing. For the farm wives, the appearance of bigger tractors and better chemicals has done away with a lot of the back-breaking, finger-curling manual labor. We are able to buy more of our foods or we eat out several times a week. We let our children get to school before they are fed. Laundry is no longer an all-day job. Few even own an iron any more. Our homes are better insulated and we no longer have to chop fire wood and keep it going. We no longer have to pile quilts on the bed to stay warm. Our homes are air conditioned and we live in a controlled environment. I have often heard some people complain about how poor they were as children growing up and how much better their family is today. But I ask, "Are we?" The children have no brothers or sisters or, if they do, most only have one or two siblings. Will they have the memories of mother cooking breakfast when they get older? Or the memories of a family pulling together and doing things together whether it be the laundry or working in the fields or garden or moms playing games at night around the table with them? So let's hope the women of today do realize how much more time they do have and how much easier it is and spend this precious "extra time" with the children. After all, that is what it is all about: love, family, and great memories.

THE LADY WITH THE FIVE GALLON BUCKET

By: Jim Ferguson

I moved to Blytheville, Arkansas in the spring of 1997. It was a new experience for me because I'd lived in Gideon, Missouri all my life except for the time I spent in the Navy. When I moved to Blytheville, I had no fishing buddies and didn't really know where to fish in the local area. However there were a couple of small lakes, Big Lake and Mallard Lake, in the vicinity. Big Lake was the tail end of the floodway ditches in southeast Missouri. I have previously written about fishing and duck hunting at the ditches. In the fall I tried Big Lake and found it to be a shallow lake that was full of lily pads and hard to get around with my big boat. I managed to catch a few fish but didn't like it much. When spring came around I ventured on over to Mallard. From what I had gathered from the locals, Mallard Lake had been drained by the University of Arkansas a few years earlier. It was to be a test lake; they were trying to make it a trophy lake for bass. At one time the state record had come from there. As a result, the locals had said there weren't any crappie in the lake and no one fished it. BIG mistake!

On my second or third trip to the lake that spring, I began catching some really big crappie and was surprised that I basically had the lake to myself with the exception of few fisherman and ladies fishing from the bank. One of those ladies is the subject of this story. On my third day at the lake, I had found a place where I caught several nice fish. On this day, when I got to the area there was an older woman sitting on a five gallon bucket on the bank fishing with a cane pole but she could not reach the spot where I'd caught all the fish the day before. So I eased on up close to my spot. Not wanting to make her feel as though I was intruding on her place, I asked her if it would be ok if I fished that particular brush pile. I continued I would give her half the fish I caught from it. Realizing this was a chance for her to go home with a mess of crappie, she was more than happy to let me fish. Just as I had thought, the fish were there. The first one I pulled out was a nice big black male crappie and I immediately tossed it to her and she put it in her bucket. Within the next ten to fifteen minutes I caught several nice fish that I shared with her on a fifty-fifty basis. Then I continued fishing up and down the lake. As I was leaving that day, she was waiting at the boat ramp and thanked me again for the fish I'd given her. We talked a few moments and parted our ways with me thinking I'd probably not see her again.

As the days and weeks passed that spring and summer, I did continue to see the lady. We always spoke when we met and I often gave her the fish I'd caught that day. As the fishing waned, I stopped going to Mallard and began to fish other places. Before long, it was hunting season and I discovered Big Lake to be an excellent duck-hunting spot that fall and winter. As the winter trudged on, I found myself anxiously awaiting spring so I could once again head to Mallard Lake to get into some more good crappie fishing. When the days were warm, I was there and, to my happy surprise, so was the lady. As she did last year, she always had her five gallon bucket and cane pole. We easily picked up where we had left off the year before--always speaking when we met and I was always giving her a mess of fish. On one occasion, it was dark by the time I reached the boat ramp but there she sat waiting for my return. She shared with me that the lady in the truck with her had wanted to go home for an hour but she had told the other woman she wasn't going until the man that drove the Dodge truck returned to the ramp. I laughed and gave her a nice mess of fish.

Later in the spring my neighbor, Joe Ward, started fishing with me. Now I had a partner to fish with but it was a learning experience for Joe because he had not fished a great deal. To his credit, he caught on quickly and was quite eager to learn, Joe and I fished Mallard Lake for several more years (along with other lakes) and caught a lot of fish and made a lot of memories. One of our favorite memories was the lady with the five gallon bucket and the cane pole. We made a habit of always giving her a mess of fish when she was present. As the years passed, it dawned on me she had become frail looking--age was catching up to the lady.

As spring approached in the year 2007, Joe and I fished together during the spring spawning season. By that time word had gotten out about the fish that were being caught from Mallard Lake causing it to become quite crowded with fishermen. That was a sad thing because Joe and I had been fishing Mallard for years as though it was our own private lake. I moved away that summer and another era of my life ended. Joe and I still fish together a few times a year, but there was something even sadder about that spring. We didn't see the lady with the five gallon bucket and the cane pole. I often wondered about her: had she died during the winter or had she just become too frail to fish any more? Another sad thing I realized was I had no way of finding out about the lady because during all the years I'd known her and talked with her, I hadn't known her name or where she lived. She was just "the lady with a five gallon bucket and a cane pole."

In memory of the lady with the five gallon bucket and the cane pole. Thanks for the memories.

SLEIGH RIDE ANYONE

By: Terry Weldon

It seemed like the Missouri winters were much worse back in the sixties, much colder and when it snowed, it would stay on the ground for four or five days. When this happened, about the second day of packed snow it was a little too risky for the school buses so we had a day out of school. One of these days I had happened to have spent the night with my cousin Wayman Baker who lived about three miles North of Gideon in a community know as "Little Walnut" after a grove of Walnut trees that stood near the road. Wayman and I were typical young men and we bored pretty quickly. We had no computers, XBOX, PS3, nor Wiis to babysit us so we had to use our imaginations. Again, we were young boys and our imaginations were fairly limited.

We were out on their farm pilfering around looking for something to get into. I spotted a 1953 Chevy hood leaning against the barn. I told Wayman, surely we can come up with something to do with that jewel. A little later we were climbing around in the barn loft wrestling in the hay. He was about fifteen years old and he had already grown to around five eleven, 220 lbs. Let's just say his seat at the dinner table was never vacant. In pretending to climb mount everest and swim across the Nile river full of piranha, it came to us like a bolt of lightening. We removed the rope from the barn loft, added an eye bolt to the front of the Chevy hood and tied the rope to it. Flipping the hood upside down, it made the perfect snow sled. We pulled it down to the ditch bank, both jumped in and headed down the slope right onto the frozen ditch. We were immediately transformed into the world's best two-man bob sled team, who would have guessed it? After two or three rides down the ditch bank and pulling the hood back to the top, we decided, it was too much for two boys, so we drug it back to the barn. Wayman, being the genius he was, came up with a brilliant idea, "let's hook the rope to the tractor". You see how his mind worked! We tied the rope securely to the tractor while I jumped in the upside down hood and down the field road we headed. After a couple of trips up and down the field road, we switched off and he rode the hood for a while. I sorta got bored with just driving on the road and thought it would be funner if I took off across the field. I was right, this was much more funner. Nearing the ditch bank, I made a hard left to head down the ridge of the bank, when I did the hood came around and passed me. This was my first lesson on centrifugal forces. I picked it up pretty fast when the thirty foot rope wrapped around the front tire of the tractor. Being young and still having quick reactions, I hit the brakes on the tractor before I damaged the hood. Once my laughter subsided, I also quickly noticed,

Wayman was no longer in the hood! I did a quick scan of the field with no luck, he wasn't any where to be found. I shut off the tractor and ran over to the crest of the bank. There he was in the fetal position on the far side of the ditch underneath some brush, not moving. Oh my God, I have killed him! He had on a pair of his dad's insulated coveralls and was looking like a tan colored polar bear. How would I explain this to Uncle Hob and Aunt Peg. As I was compiling a story, he rolled over and tears were running down his cheeks from the laughter. He crawled up the ditch bank and said, "Let's do that again".

I decided I had gotten my blood pressure high enough for a guy my age, so we went back to the house and had two bologna sandwiches and a tall glass of milk, each. We were so excited about the new game we had invented, we had to tell someone our age, so we filled up the tractor and headed into Gideon. Coming across three ditch bridge on the North end of town, we made a left and started down in front of Hilfiker's grocery store where we picked up Jamer Hilfiker, continuing on we crossed the railroad tracks where they had cleared the snow. With sparks flying from the hood dragging over the rocks and railroad tracks, me an Jamer went airborne for a few seconds. Just past Elam's store Ronnie Lowery and two girls came aboard. Remember this was a 1953 Chevy hood. It would hold at least eight kids, ten if you stacked then; which we did! Making a right at the next street we eased over to main street, after he stopped and let everyone back on the sled from being slung off turning the corner. We turned left on Main St going South toward the school.

Gaining Kent Reynolds and Jack Utterback at the Western Auto without slowing down we were getting pretty good at this stuff. Further South around the Methodist church, we picked up Tater Cahill and Toby Jordan.

We decided it wouldn't be smart to take the tractor onto the school grounds, so we turned left and headed for the ball park just East of town in front of my house. Passing Davis' grocery a new friend, (perfect stranger), jumped on board, now we were beginning to stack them. We lost a few going over the railroad tracks in front of McChord's gin, stopped, restacked and continued on. Once we were out in the open field by the ballpark, the fun really began. There were even a couple of maneuvers that ended up with the sled half way up the outfield fence. Kids were scattered all over the ballfield. If you were thrown off, the tractor would not stop, you had to get back on the best you could.

Right when we were all sweating in the twenty five degree weather, Bo Wingo, the local police, came driving up! None of us were old enough to drive, so how were we supposed to know that was illegal...

THE LAST OF THE COWBOYS

By: Jim Ferguson

Once again I am going back to my childhood to a time and place that had a lot of influence on me--my grandparent's home in Wilburn, a small town in Arkansas. I first wrote about it in the story "Summer at Grannie's." As I mentioned, going there in the mid- and late fifties was like stepping back in time. The roads were gravel, water was drawn from a well, baths were either taken in a tub or in the creek, and wood was burned in the winter to heat the home and the store that my grandfather ran. Customers arrived at the store on a wagon pulled by a team of horses which were tied to the hitching post in front of the store. Since I was a young kid who was very much into watching and playing cowboys, it was a great place to be. The reason I'm going back to that era of my life is I would like to introduce and tell you about a man I have known my entire life. A man who became a hero to me. My first remembrance of him was when he rode across the road on his horse to my grandfather's store. As I stood there looking up to him with awe, he looked down and said, "You must be Sissy's boy." WOW! A real cowboy was talking to me. Now I don't remember if I said anything in return or if I just ran off but I do remember the exchange. That man is H. L .Stonewalter. H.L., born in 1934, was raised across the road from where my mother was raised and went to school with her, her sisters, and her nephews. They played on Slate Hill, waded and swam in the creeks, and worked in the fields together as all the kids did in that era. One of my first memories of H.L. is his giving me a ride on his horse one night. I have forgotten the reason for the ride, but he came by my grandmother's house early one night looking for my mom and dad. They had gone down the road "apiece" to visit one of my great aunts. H. L. just reached down, offered me a hand, and pulled me onto the saddle behind him and off we went. Although I had ridden hundreds of miles on my stick horse, this was the first time I had ever been on a real horse and I have remembered that night well over fifty years. I don't think I will ever forget it. The clip-clop of the horse's hoofs was exciting to me as we cantered down the road to my great aunt's house. At the time, neither H. L. nor I realized that this one ride on this dark night would bind us to a friendship that would last a lifetime. As the years passed and I aged, I always returned to my grandmother's house a couple of times a year. I always saw and visited with H. L. often getting the opportunity to ride his horses or help him put the summer hay into the barn so he would have feed for his cattle and horses during the winter months. He taught me how to use a rope to lasso the cattle. In my eyes he was a true cowboy--not like the ones you see today walking around with the snakeskin boots and their hundred dollar hats. H. L.'s boots were scuffed and scarred from long days of labor that he spent working around the farm. The ole hat he wore was stained with sweat from the hours of hard work in the hot sun. His hands were callused from years of throwing hay bales into the loft of the barn. Yes he was a true working cowboy. As the years continued to pass, we maintained our friendship after I married and we would continue to visit the area where my grandmother had lived. My mother and dad moved back to the old home place in the early eighties and I would always drop by to see H. L. There was always plenty of strong coffee in the pot or fresh cow's milk to drink. Conversation was always easy whether we were talking about my two boys or talking about the eleven kids that he and his wife, Clara, raised. Or I would listen with envy as they would tell of the trail rides they were always going on and the rodeos they attended or of their trips to Colorado. Another favorite of mine was listening to H. L. tell of his dream of someday saddling his horse and riding him all the way to Colorado and camping out along the way. On one of our trips in the late seventies, I mentioned that someday I would like to move to that part of the country. H.L. responded that his sister had a piece of land for sale down on the river not far from him that I could buy cheap. We looked at it and talked about buying it but, being young and dumb and not having the foresight, we decided not to buy it. That same piece of land today is worth a fortune. If I had only listened to my ole friend... But as always time changes all things. H. L. is 78 years and I am almost sixty. He never got to make his trip to Colorado on horseback because he was in a serious accident a few years ago. It almost killed him. He lost a leg and is no longer able to ride horses. He and Clara still live on the old home place and I still visit them whenever I'm in the area. If you ever go through Wilburn, Arkansas, stop by and visit the Stonewalters. There will be strong coffee to drink and stories of the past to be heard. To you my ole friend who lived by the code of a cowboy, I tip my Stetson to you. YOU ARE THE LAST OF THE COWBOYS. THANKS FOR THE MEMORIES

THE MAN IN GREEN

By: Jim Ferguson

While living in Blytheville, Arkansas I spent a lot of time fishing for crappie on Mallard Lake. Since the lake had a lot of nice crappie, I often did quite well in the early spring and would catch my limit easily. However crappie wasn't the only fish Mallard had in it. It also had large mouth bass and they were the pets of the Arkansas Game and Fish Department. I say they were their pets because they have strict procession rules on them. For instance, you were only allowed one per day in procession and it had to be over 22 inches long but less than 25 inches long. The purpose for this size limit was the Arkansas Fish and Game was trying to make Mallard a trophy bass lake. On one of my outings at Mallard I had caught my limit of crappie early. On the way back home I stopped at a bait shop a mile or so away from the lake to get a soda and something to eat. While I was at the bait shop a man and his young son who had also stopped there to get some bait asked if I had caught any fish. I told them I had and asked the young boy if he would like to see them. Excitedly, he hopped in my boat to see the fish in the live well. As the young boy was looking at the fish I heard another truck pull up. Turning around I could see it was "The Man in Green"--an Arkansas Game and Fish Agent (game warden) who also asked if he could see my fish. I told him, "Sure, I'm quite proud of them." He was impressed and complimented me on my catch stating they were some really nice crappie. However he asked if he could take the one bass I had out of the live well so he could get a better look at it. Now having been down this road before with the Men in Green, I knew he was up to something. He continued and asked if I knew how long it was. I told him I guessed it to be close to twenty inches or so. He then asked if I minded if he measured it. I responded that he could but I would like to know why he wanted to measure the bass. He stated there is a size limit for bass that come from Mallard Lake. I asked him what that had to do with this particular bass since it didn't come from Mallard Lake. He then asked me where I caught it to which I replied Big Lake. (The two lakes set side by side with only a levy separating them and both have boat ramps making it easy for fisherman to fish either lake.) Not liking my answer he asked if I had caught all these fish in Big Lake. The answer I gave him was "No." Then I explained that I first started fishing this morning in Big Lake but after fishing for awhile and only catching this bass, I loaded my boat back onto the trailer and re-launched it into Mallard Lake which is where I caught the crappie. After my explanation, I could see by the look on his face that this conversation wasn't going the way he had intended for it to go. He then said, "Sir, I think you are lying to me." Now in a lot of cases that would get a fellow punched right in the old nose but being a little wiser than I was in my youth (or even a day or two ago) I just informed "The Man in Green" that I saw no reason for us to stand here arguing over this. If he thought he had enough evidence and could make it stick, then he should just write me a ticket. However since we were away from the lake and he hadn't seen where I was fishing, I didn't think it would hold up in court but the decision was up to him. He tossed the bass back into my boat and walked away looking at the registration on my boat as he passed it. After "The Man in Green" left, I also looked at the registration and saw this was the last day for it to be valid. After returning home and cleaning my fish, I went to the county court house and got the new stickers for my boat which proved to be a very smart thing to do. The next morning as I was launching my boat "The Man in Green" pulled up and climbed out of his truck with his ticket book in hand. He walked straight to me, looked at the boat, and realized I had replaced the sticker with a new one. I could just see the wind escape from him. I then thanked him for noticing yesterday that my registration was expired because if he hadn't done so, I may not have seen it for weeks. Once again I could tell he didn't like the way things were going. He asked me for my fishing licenses and registration papers. Then he checked my boat for life jackets, fire extinguisher, whistle, and throwable floatation device and found all things in order. He left and I continued on my way fishing. I noticed he kept driving around the lake several times that morning and, as I expected, when I came to the boat ramp later --here he was waiting for me. He checked my fish, fire extinguisher, whistle, life jackets, throwable device, and licenses and registration papers again. This process continued for the next three days whenever I launched in the morning and when I returned. After he checked me on the third day, I informed him that if he was here the next day, I would be making a call to someone to file a complaint for harassment. To my surprise the next morning he never showed up nor did I see him again until a couple weeks later. He showed up with five other agents. My first thoughts were he had brought reinforcements and I was in trouble. However I wasn't their concern that day since they were busy shocking fish, counting, measuring and putting them into a huge live well. As they came past me I couldn't help saying to them, "That's a pretty lazy way to get a mess of fish." The look on the face of the game warden was priceless! The facts to this story are true and as follows. Number one: I did catch the crappie out of Mallard Lake. Number two:

the man and young boy were impressed with the fish. Number three: "The Man in Green" wasn't so impressed but he couldn't prove that I caught the bass out of Mallard Lake. Number Four: as to where I did catch the bass--I'll let you decide on that.

Thanks for the memories to "The Man in Green."

THE FLATBED

By: Terry Weldon

I started school at Gideon Elementary with the same people I graduated with. A few came and went, but for the most it was the same core of classmates throughout my school days.

Each person was a special friend for a different reason. One of those friends later in my school day was Dennis Skidmore. Dennis was a real competitor in everything he did. He was a natural athlete and excelled in all of them. He ran in track and field in school and held several of the athletic records for a while in high school. I, on the other hand was a little small to compete with him, but there was one thing I could do, "set ups". Because of my size and physique I could do set ups until you got tired counting. When we were in high school, I wanted to be on that records board so badly I would have paid the judges. But I didn't. I saw the record board and every other name was Dennis Skidmore. I went after the set ups record, thinking he didn't care much about that one, however, Dennis cared about them all. I took the record for setups; I don't remember how many I did, but it was in the hundreds, his name came down and my name went up. Proud as a peacock, and cocky as one to, I really rubbed it in to Dennis. The very next month, he beat my record. Friends are friends and competitors are competitors, next month I took it back. Coach Brawner really enjoyed this type of competition and he coaxed it on. Coming down to the end of our school year Dennis took it back and there wasn't enough time for me to try again before school was out. I didn't want to leave school without my name on that board, but it wasn't to be. However, I did receive the "PhysEd" award that year. I think it was out of pity, but I didn't care what the reason, Dennis didn't get it!

Just before school was out there was some talk of getting rid of "Senior skip day", of course they would during our Senior year. Dennis Skidmore, Kent Reynolds, Ron Lowery, James Pickard, and myself decided we might be able to influence that decision. One Friday we made sure the science room window was left unlocked, that night we went out and gathered up, possums, turtles, some chickens, and two snakes. We opened the window to the science room and deposited all these critters, making sure the door to the hallway was left open and the game was free to roam. Our thought pattern was they would let school out Monday while they cleared out the school not knowing how many were loose inside, clever uh?. Some more of that Forrest Gump thinking, stupid is as stupid does, and we all actually graduated. Little did we know the Janitors came in sometimes on the weekends. They simply opened the doors and let all of the critters out. Then they stood back Monday morning and looked out for guys that looked like Forrest Gump. I am sure we stood out like a sore thumb. We tied one of the snakes to the chain on the flagpole, (really funny in 1967), but the custodians refused to take it down. Someone, (not me), Dennis I think, snitched on James Pickard and he had to take it down.

Dennis had many girlfriends throughout his high school years, but one stands out in my memory; ole' what's her name. It was her birthday and Dennis wanted to do something special, so he came to me for ideas. He came to the right person, I had a great idea. I had recently seen a wedding where they released these beautiful white doves just before the couple left the church. We didn't have white doves, but I had a barn full of pigeons. Dennis came over that night, we caught ten pigeons, some of which were white, the next day we waited until school was over and everyone was gone, but the doors weren't locked. We sneaked in and placed those pigeons in her locker. Then, the next morning she would open her locker and "SURPRISE". This was a near- brilliant idea if I do say so myself. The next morning Dennis and I parked ourselves just around the corner from ole' what's her names locker and waited for the "Grand Opening". It couldn't have went any better, she opened the locker and out the birds came. The hallway was packed with kids and it might as well been everyone's birthday, because they all got a big surprise. We watched as she stood there in total amazement, she was just staring into her locker and then she started to cry. Something had went wrong with this surprise. Dennis and I ran over to her and what we didn't think about had happened. Those pigeons had crapped all over everything in her locker, ruining her books, tennis shoes and gym clothes. I turned to Dennis and said, "I told you this was a dumb idea".

Dennis' parents always treated me like one of their own when I went to visit. Dennis had chores to do. If he had done them, we could take their pickup truck out on the weekends. One Friday night there was a special function with two knock-out dates and we sort of had to dress up. I actually don't remember the two girls, but they were foreigners, from way over in Malden, Missouri. For some reason Dennis had not done his chores, I am sure he had a very good reason. When it was time to go, he asked his dad for the truck keys. His dad said, sorry you didn't finish your chores. He said to unload the flatbed truck full of hay bales and stack them under the pole barn. We had backed the flatbed under the pole barn and planned to unload it in the morning, however, his dad had a different idea, namely, do it now! We began tossing that hay for all we were worth. The darker it got, the harder we threw them. We planned to come back and straighten them out the next morning. After telling his dad we were finished, he decided to check our work because we were a little too energetic. He came out, saw bales of hay all over the place and said, sorry boys, no truck. We begged, but he was a little upset with us and told us if we just had to go out that evening, we could take the flatbed, thinking we would be so embarrassed, we wouldn't go. This old rust bucket was held together by Missouri gumbo and baling wire. It hadn't had water on it since we drove it into the road ditch the month before. Being the men that we were, we didn't back down, we jumped in the flatbed and took off. We took these two girls to their homecoming football at

Malden where everyone in town could see us. We never saw those two girls again. I told Dennis it was a dumb idea!

THE MEN WHO SAVED AMERICA

By: Jim Ferguson

The time was the early 1920s and things were going pretty good in America. The era was known as the "roaring twenties." World War I was over and the influenza that swept the world killing millions was subsiding. Factory orders were picking up, new farm land was being cleared across the United States, and babies were being born. Little did the mothers and fathers of these babies know that it would be their sons who would be called upon within twenty years to take on a task like none other. One of these babies was my dad, Ralph Ferguson. Dad and hundreds of thousand of American boys like him would set their shoulders to accomplish this task before they reached the age of twenty-five. But first they would have to be tempered like steel--made hard and strong. This was partly done by the crash of the stock market in 1929 which caused the Great Depression to spread across the United States and the rest of the world. Times became hard, no jobs could be found in the cities, and soup lines and starvation were every-day business in some areas of the country. In the rural areas, young boys had to quit school just to help make a living for the family. They went to work with their dads on the farms or the logging camps. This is what my dad did; he worked with my grandfather making rail road ties. They used a crosscut saw to fell the tree, an ax to trim it, and a broad ax to form it into ties. I have that old broad axe today hanging on the mantle of my fireplace. As the depression dragged on into the late thirties, President Roosevelt formed what would be called the CC Camps. These were job corps projects run by the government for the purpose of putting the young American boys back to work. They built schools, roads, bridges, and other projects. The camps were run on a military basis and the boys lived in barracks on camps spread across the nation. A lot of the camps were self-sufficient. The men were trained in all areas from welders to carpenters to cooks. That is where my dad learned to bake--the skill that would define his job in the Navy a couple of years later when, on December 7, 1941, Japan bombed Pearl Harbor. With a war already raging in Europe, the United States declared war on Japan. Germany, an ally of Japan, then declared war on the United States which set the stage for World War II. It also sealed the fate of hundreds of thousands of American men. The same men who were born in the late teens and early twenties were now drafted into the service to become combat troops for the Army, Navy, Army Air Corps, and Marines. They left the farms and cities across this country and traveled to all parts of the earth to fight and die for the very existence of this country and for the freedom of the rest of the men and women of the world. My dad was one of those men. He served in the South Pacific aboard the *U.S.S. Wabash* and the *USS McKinley*. He survived many battles and attacks from the Japanese. After the ending of the war, Dad was still serving on the *USS McKinley* when it took part in "Operation Crossroads," an operation which took place on a small atoll in the Marshall Islands. The purpose of the operation was to test the atomic bomb. The Defense Department wanted to study the effects of the bomb on ships, the islands, and the surrounding waters. Forty years later Dad became sick and during a visit to a doctor in Memphis he was asked if he was ever around any radiation. He responded that he had been exposed while serving in the Navy during World War II. To this the doctor replied that it would be the cause of his death. Even with that in mind, Dad was one of the lucky men of World War II. Hundreds of thousands died. Many more came home crippled while others came home "shell shocked" and suffering from what we know today as post traumatic stress disorder. Most came home healthy and able to put the war behind them. They created jobs and raised big families causing the economy of the United States to boom. I was born in 1952. Although I worked hard as a kid, I was still blessed by the heroics of these men who saved a nation and made it better for the next generation to follow. I never went hungry like many of them did during the depression. The conditions in which I was raised were far better than what they had as kids growing up during the depression. I owe a lot to them. As Tom Brokaw has said, they are the "Greatest Generation." That is the reason tears were brought to my eyes thirty years later while driving to work one cold winter afternoon. I picked up a hitch hiker (something that I've done quite often). The man who was around my dad's age was wearing an old overcoat. His shoes looked worn out and he had the appearance of not having shaved in a few days. The odor of alcohol was also on his breath. When I asked where he was headed he told me the name of a town that was close to my work place. As we drove along, I told him I was headed to work to which he replied, "That is a good thing; a man needs a job"--something he said he was never able to keep. He asked me if I was ever in the military and I told him, "Yes." He replied he was too at one time and even won some medals. Reaching into the inner part of his coat, he pulled out a case that was worn by the many years of being carried and handled. When I saw what was inside the box, I pulled my truck to the side of the road. Inside the box being held by the shaky hands of this old man lay three medals: a Purple Heart, a Silver Star, and the Medal of Honor. I was stunned and amazed. I had seen the Purple Heart and the Silver Star before because I had a brother-in-law who earned them in Viet Nam. The only Medal of Honor I had ever seen was in pictures. He told me he had earned them fighting against the Germans in World War II. To this day I believe him after seeing the pride in his eyes. Since then I often have wondered how a man who fought hard enough to win those medals could not defeat the ghosts of his past causing him to wind up in his current situation. We all know that war is hell and some men can move forward while others are unable to do so. Even those who can not are and should be honored as "One of the Men Who Saved America."

I salute you, Sir!

THE RUNWAYS

By: Jim Ferguson

I often remember leaning on my hoe handle as a young boy and watching the airplanes fly overhead while they practiced their flight skills as they flew in and out of the air base in Malden, Missouri during the mid-fifties, or watching the crop dusters Like John Huie or others take off from the runways at the Gideon Airport. While delivering the chemicals to the crops, they would often get so low the wheels of the plane would brush the tops of the crops they were spraying. I was dreaming of how exciting it would be to be flying inside the cockpit becoming an ace shooting down enemy pilots or bombing enemy targets instead of on the ground chopping cotton in the hot summer. My dreams were always interrupted by the hoe being kicked out from under me or the sound of my mother telling me to get busy and stop day dreaming (a habit I have been cursed with my entire life). As the days of my youth faded away into the past so did the dreams of becoming a pilot as I spent too much time fishing the ditches and looking for Indian relics and not spending enough time studying. The idea of flying was after all just the dream of a dreamer. That was probably a good thing for I never rode or drove anything--be it a bicycle, car or motorcycle--without taking it to the limits which isn't a good thing to do if you are flying. When flying planes you often don't get a second chance. But as always time changes all things. I may not have ever learned to fly but I have had my fun on the runways.

During the mid-seventies, a friend of mine, Chuck Holiman, who had made several jumps from airplanes, came up with the idea one Sunday morning that he and I should take his parachute and a long rope to the airport. Upon our arrival, we attached one end of the rope to my jeep and the other end to the harness of the parachute that he was wearing. Putting the jeep in gear I headed down the runway with Chuck running behind me until the chute filled with air then became airborne (redneck parasailing). After pulling Chuck for a half a mile or so and noticing that he was hanging kind of limp, I reduced my speed and he gently returned to earth. But instead of standing up he just wilted and lay on the runway. By the time I reached him he was coming to. Apparently the harness had slipped and was choking him and causing him to black out. Good thing I checked on him when I did; may have been hard to explain the cause of death. Deciding that we needed to modify the harness we suspended our runway activities for the day.

As the days and years passed I once again found myself on the runways of the Gideon Airport but this time with my boys and several other boys from Gideon. It was a cold winter day and we had several inches of snow. With that in mind and adding a rope, a sled, and three wheelers you can see there could be a lot of fun and thrills in the future. And it was--as long as I was the adult doing the pulling of the sled. Now I do have to admit I gave the boys a good ride. I wasn't too easy on them but, after all, they were young and healed fast. The problem was these boys. I coached little league baseball for them, played a little basketball with them, and took them rabbit hunting. Therefore I guess it didn't occur to them that I don't heal as quickly as they did. This being said: they could hardly wait until they got their turn pulling me on the sled behind the three wheeler. Now the boy who drew the lucky straw and became the driver was Kelly Gains. Kelly was one of those boys that you would think was really a nice quiet boy and always had a smile on his face. You might even think you could trust the kid; however you were taking your life in your hands if you did. Behind that smile and gentle eyes was a boy who was always thinking and scheming. After the first hundred feet behind the three wheeler with him driving, I knew I had once again made a miscalculation and was in for the ride of my life. After hanging on and surviving a few turns I thought, "Well I'm going to make it through this." But that just seemed to fuel the fire in Kelly as he became more determined to throw me off the sled. Gaining speed as he went down the runway he crossed from one side to the other setting me up for a whip action. As he made his turn I gained speed and managed to maintain my grip until the last moment when I knew this is going to hurt. I came off the sled with lightning speed, became airborne, and landed off the runway and rolled across several yards of plowed ground. Of course, the breath was knocked out of me. I was still lying on the ground when Kelly came back to check on me. Now I'm not saying he was laughing but when I looked he had a huge grin across his face. However I suffered no broken bones and was able to walk on my own even though I was sore for several days. We had a lot of fun on the runways and memories were made. Kelly still laughs to this day about that ride. My only prayer is someday a young kid will treat him to the same adventure and get revenge for me. Chuck, like me, is getting older and we are both a little bit wiser but we have a lifetime of memories.

Thanks for the memories, boys.

THE MAN

By: Terry Weldon

It was the 7th grade, my first year in the high school building and I was somebody now! Loren Stephens, Kent Reynolds, and Vicky Jordan had dared me to run to the back of the boiler to see what was back there. I was no coward nor could I pass up a dare. I eased the door open, listening for some form of life in there then tip toed inside. It was larger than life back then. I would have thought you could heat the entire city of Gideon with that boiler. I continued toward the back to see what mysteries lie in wait for me. Once I got there all I saw was a couple of dust coats and some brooms and mops. Quite a let down at the time. I turned to report back to my crew and there he was, 6 feet 6 inches, 230 pounds, built like a lumber Jack, at least that is the way I saw Vernon Tolbert for the first time. For those of you that know Vernon, I might have been a little off on his size, regardless, he was "The Man" and I had been caught on his turf. Before he could say hello and ask what I needed, I was out of there like a flash, trying to blend into the crowd while heading for my next class.

As the months went by I saw Vernon again as he was sweeping the hallway, every time we made eye contact, he gave me the "evil eye", like he knew it was me that time in the boiler room. He had changed in size somewhat, but he was still "The Man" and I had to stay out of his way or get on good terms with him somehow. By the eighth grade I was an old timer around the high school, I had even talked a few 7th graders into going into the back of the boiler room.

As an eighth grader, we started using the "new gym" for Physical Education (PE). Of course it was known all over the New Madrid and three adjoining counties that NO ONE walked on the gym floor with street shoes, no exceptions.

One day just at the end of PE class, the coach was called to the office which was in the main building. We finished our class and headed for the showers. After our showers we were standing by the bleachers waiting for the bell to ring when one of my "good friends" dared me to try my hand at a free throw because he knew I would never have a chance at a shot from the sidelines. I thought, I could probably make a free throw and I had on my U.S. Keds which were not really street shoes. I strolled out onto the court took a couple of bounces with the ball and with all I had from my 4 foot 6 inch physique away the ball went. I would say it was about five feet from being the best free throw in that gym ever, when who walked around the corner and said "nice shot", Vernon Tolbert! How could this happen twice? At this point he was bigger than I thought. I knew custodians couldn't spank students, but he was still "The Man" and I did push the broom for the next four PE classes.

I did make it to the 9th grade which means you are nobody. No longer Jr high, but not quite high school. We were always looking for some way of getting attention and I was no different than the rest. One beautiful summer day we were all outside for lunch when one of my "good friends" dared me to run up one of the beams of the new gym and over the top and down the beam on the other side. Do you see a pattern here? Yes, I did, and Yes Vernon Tolbert was on the other side waiting for me. This is the time I learned how to wax the floor of the gym!

Sophomore year came and we were somebody again, one of the high school kids finally. Halloween that year was a gloomy night, winter was a little early and it was drizzling rain. Several of us gathered in the parking lot behind the school. Everyone had a couple of rolls of toilet paper. You could throw those things really high and they would trail over those trees perfectly. We had all thrown our rolls and were hurrying to get out of there, as we rounded the corner of the building I found a roll that hadn't been used, I grabbed it and chunked it over the tallest tree when I heard a voice from a dark corner of the building say "Nice throw". You guessed it, Vernon Tolbert! Because he was "The Man", I spent the next day with a water hose washing all of that toilet paper out of those trees.

Junior year I had begun trade school where we went to school at Gideon and caught another bus to school on the Air Base at Malden, then back to Gideon for the afternoon classes. I was excited about this adventure until I got to school and found the bus to trade school and there he was, Vernon Tolbert was the driver. Why was I being punished, I never dated or even hit on any of his daughters, and he had plenty of them. All went well the first couple of months until I got caught smoking on the bus, then I rode in the front seat the rest of the year.

My senior year came and my life changed. My Grandparents, P.O. and Dollie Beasley, who had lived in the same house across the road from the ballpark at Gideon, Missouri since I was one year old, had a house built in Clarkton Missouri. We had no car and I couldn't possibly go to school my senior year at Clarkton. When Vernon Tolbert heard about my problem, he changed the route he drove to trade school and picked me up at Clarkton every morning of my senior year allowing me to finish school where I started, Gideon High, Class of 68'. Vernon Tolbert, you are "The Man".

THREE BOYS AND A SCOOTER

By: Jim Ferguson

Most of my youth was spent in the cotton fields since my dad was a farmer. We chopped all of our own cotton and, when we finished with ours, we would hire out to other farmers in the area to make money for school clothes. When we weren't working in the fields, there were two places you could always bet I could be found. One would be hunting Indian relics on several mounds that were scattered across southeast Missouri. The mounds were built by Native Americans who were called "The Mound Builders." Around 1000 A.D. to 1300 A.D. they were built along the many sloughs and swamps up and down the Mississippi River Valley. Most of those sloughs and swamps have been drained as a result of the building of The Floodway Drainage System. However, the mounds can still be found by their higher elevation and the darker color of the soil. The other place I could be found is fishing in one of those ditches. Now, unlike most days I spent fishing, this day is a little different. Carl Blackwood (alias Jughead) and I spent the night with a friend of ours, Rick Roberts. After staying up late the night before making our plans for the next day, we woke early the next morning and ate the breakfast Mrs. Roberts prepared for us. After eating we left the house, grabbed a couple shovels and a coffee can from the shed. Then we headed to our worm bed to gather our bait for the day. Within thirty minutes we had dug enough worms to fill the coffee can half full of the biggest, fattest, juiciest worms three boys could dig. After filling up the rest of the can with good damp dirt, we were ready to get the rest of our things. Now my fishing equipment was the best there was at the time. I have an aunt who worked for Heddin Lure Company in Michigan and each year she would bring me all the newest rods and reels plus an abundant supply of bass lures. Since I was not a bass fisherman but rather leaned more to catfish and perch, I removed all the hooks from the bass lures and put the hooks in my tackle box. I threw the lures away. Looking back, I realize I should have kept them because today those lures are worth a lot of money.

Having collected all our gear we were now ready to leave. Most days, we would walk to our fishing spot. But not today! Since Rick got a motor scooter for his birthday, we were going like big dogs. We were riding. After deciding where and how we were all going to ride on the scooter, we headed out--three boys, nine poles, three tackle boxes, a can of worms, and three canteens. Why we took the canteens I haven't a clue because we drank water out of those ditches plenty of times before. It's a wonder we didn't die drinking that water.

Upon leaving Rick's house we had to travel on a black topped road for a mile before turning west onto a county road which was gravel. Then we had to go another two miles before we reached Number Two Ditch where our day of fishing would take place. However, as things have always seemed to go for me in my life, before reaching the gravel road we had a problem. We met a Missouri Highway Patrolman who quickly made a "U" turn and gave chase. With us barely doing thirty-five miles per hour. We soon found ourselves sitting on the side of the road with the patrolman asking Rick for his driver's license. Since we were obviously not over eleven or twelve years of age I don't know why he would ask that. Routine, I guess. After giving us a good scolding laced with the threat of being hauled off to jail, the patrolman released us and made us promise we would return home and not get back onto the road again with the scooter. We were very glad to do so. Parking the scooter and not saying a word to Rick's mother, we walked to Number Three Ditch which was directly behind Rick's house where we spent the rest of the day fishing and fussing about the patrolman. It has been almost fifty years since that day. Where Rick Roberts is, I haven't a clue but the last I heard he lived in Memphis, Tennessee. As for Carl Blackwood, I still see him and fish with him on occasion. The patrolman would be well into his seventies now if he is still alive. I'd bet on days that he looks back upon his life he still thinks and laughs about the Three Boys on a Scooter.

Thanks to all for the memories.

TRAPS

By: Jim Ferguson

One of the earliest means of supplying the family or
the clan with food has always been the use of traps.
You could set several which would increase your
chance of catching something. Now as a young boy I
was always seeing this done on TV. They would
catch rabbits, beaver, muskrats, birds, and in some
shows they would even show catching people. Now
being the kid that I was, this was always interesting
to me. I have tried all the ways there were to catch
game and have experienced some success at it. My
dad showed me how to build rabbit box traps the
way he did as a young boy. And I managed to catch
a few rabbits. With them, the hardest part was
killing the rabbits after you had caught them in the
trap. You can't just reach in with your hand and
grab them because they will bite. I learned that the
hard way and still have a scar on my thumb to prove
it. I learned to shake them into a burlap bag where I
could then take a hammer or a rock and whack them
in the head. Now even though they were called
rabbit traps I would often catch other critters in it. I
have caught possums, rats, squirrels, and even
caught a cat once. Now you want to see something--
try getting a cat out of a trap after it has been pinned
up for a few hours. They are not in a good mood at
all! Other traps I have used are bird traps. I have
tried to catch birds a lot of times by propping a box
up with a stick and then pulling the stick out from
under it when birds went under the box to feed and,
therefore, trapping the bird. I have seen this done
several times on TV but I never had any luck doing
it. However, my Uncle Alex once showed me how to

build a bird trap out of chicken wire and I caught a lot of quail with it. He also showed me how to build one by digging a hole in the ground and covering it with a tarp, rug, or even a piece of cardboard. To do this, dig a hole about two feet square and eight to twelve inches deep. Starting about one to two feet away from the hole, dig a ramp leading to the hole. The next step is to cover the hole and <u>half</u> of the ramp with the cardboard or whatever you plan to use to cover it. In the middle of the covering cut a small, three-inch hole or whatever will work--big enough to let sunlight in but not big enough a quail can get through. Then you just simply throw some corn or wheat seed in and around the ramp. The quail will follow the seeds into the hole. Instead of coming back up the ramp, they will try flying out the hole through the covering. Since they are unable to fly out, they will be waiting for you when you return. However let me suggest if you try this, always raise one corner of the covering to check your trap before just sticking your hand in because sometimes a snake will go in also to eat the birds. One other thing: instead of just going somewhere and building this trap, first find where the coveys of quail are feeding and then build it. "It will work." I have caught several quail this way and have often caught the whole covey. Do remember to release part of the catch so the covey can continue to thrive in the area. I have also used fish traps (as have other people throughout history). They can also be made of wire (welded fence wire) and it will work. The best ones I ever used were made of wood. They would be either square or round and four to five feet long with a throut built in one end which allows the fish to enter but they are unable to come back out. They are trapped. I always baited mine with rotten cheese which catfish love. I have caught hundreds of fish with these traps. Often the trap would be filled the first night it was set. Knowing how to set traps and use them came in handy once after I was grown. My brother-in-law John and I decided to raise some pigs. After throwing them into the pen the first afternoon we had one to escape. Since the surrounding area was farm ground and the crops were tall, that pig managed to stay loose for several weeks--even months. Often Dad or one of the neighbors would see it crossing the road or on the edge of the fields. As fall approached and Dad began to gather the crops, it became clear that if we didn't soon do something the hog would be leaving the area where he was staying. I came up with an idea on how to catch this hog. After telling Dad of my plan he gave me a huge laugh and said it could not be done. However not giving me a better solution than riding the combine with him and hoping to get a shot at it, I continued with my plan of attack. I had a huge rabbit cage at home that wasn't being used so I began to modify it. I cut the legs off so it would sit on the ground and removed the small door and made it bigger. I made it similar to the rabbit traps with a trap door that I had made as a young boy. I set my trap in place one afternoon and baited it with scraps of food all the while having to listen to Dad laugh about my plan. I had confidence that it would work. After all if you could catch a rabbit why could you not catch a hog? Same principle but just with a bigger trap and better built. It made complete sense to me. And to Dad's surprise, I caught the hog the first night. Mission accomplished, right? Well sometimes it's the little things that cause problems.

When John and I went to lift the trap into the back of the truck to transport the hog to the pen, we forgot to nail the door to the cage shut. When we lifted the cage, the door opened and the hog ran out. Once again the hog was loose and, once again, Dad was laughing. Now being a little "pig headed" myself, I reset the trap and baited it again knowing hogs couldn't be that smart. Just as I expected, I caught the hog the next night. You can be sure that this time we nailed the door shut and put rings in his nose so he couldn't root out. We returned the hog to the pen where he stayed until he was fat enough to be transformed into ham, bacon and pork chops. Dad and I laughed for years about that hog! Many times when I had a plan for doing something and Dad told me it wouldn't work, I always reminded him of "The Hog Trap."

Trapped Memories.

UNCLE SMOKEY

By: Terry Weldon

I was raised by my granny and Grandpa Beasley, my mother's parents. They had eleven children of their own. When my mother passed away, granny and Grandpa never hesitated to continue raising me, my brother and sister. I was four years old when mom passed and granny and grandpa Beasley had three or four children still at home, one of which was "Uncle Smokey". He was nine years older than me and I looked up to him to set the example, not very smart on my part. My brother and I were living with granny and grandpa Beasley, therefore he and

Smokey would fight and wrestle every minute of every day from 1954 through 1956. I hated it when my brother went to live with our dad, because that left me an easy target for Uncle Smokey. He would expend more energy getting me to do his chores than it would have taken to do the chore himself. Although I didn't want to see him harmed, I was very happy when he left for the Air Force. That left me and Aunt Margie at home and I could pretty much out run her.

One summer Uncle Smokey came home on leave from the Air Force he was a little low on money, so he thought he would chop a little cotton one Saturday morning to make a few extra dollars. He grabbed a hoe from the back porch and took off across the fields. It was one of those days where the sun was shining and the sky was crystal clear. One hour later an electrical storm came through and it was raining so hard you couldn't see ten feet in front of you. Granny and I was standing on the porch watching it storm and hoping Uncle Smokey had found a safe place to get out of the way of the lightening. In what was the hardest rain and the most lightening of the storm, we heard some one whistling, yes, whistling. We could barely see someone coming down the driveway, it was Uncle Smokey, with hoe handle over his shoulder, like the returning warrior, whistling to the top of his lungs.

The next summer Uncle Smokey was home on leave again during cotton chopping time. It was a Saturday and I could go to town when I had finished chopping "Ann's patch", which was a couple of acres. I asked Uncle Smokey if he would give me a hand and he agreed. I was astonished! I thought to myself, the

Air Force has been really good for him. I sharpened our hoes and when he got up around 9:00am, he came out to the field to help me. I told him to go over to the other side of the field and start back toward me. We would meet in the middle and I would be off for the day. He went over to the last row and started chopping. When he got to the other end of the row, near the railroad trestle, I saw him stop and was staring up at something. I couldn't see what he was looking at, so I assumed it was something in the trees along the railroad track. I continued chopping over to where he was, only to discover he had chopped one row of cotton, stood his hoe up in a mound of dirt and placed his cap on top of it, pointing toward the trees. He had crossed the trestle and gone to town. I didn't see him until the next day. Today, I'm told I could pass for Uncle Smokey's twin. I hope they mean by looks only!

Love you Uncle Smokey...

UGLY

By: Jim Ferguson

As you have read in one of my other stories, the rumor is I came into this world starving to death and I will say that is probably more of a fact than a rumor. However there is another rumor about that historical day and that rumor is that I was a pretty baby. That, my friend, is a downright lie but, at least, it was told so as not to hurt my feelings. I have always had a great memory for minute details. Admittedly, I misused this talent by not taking advantage of it in the classroom. However I can remember all the good fishing spots in dozens of lakes and can tell you how many fish I caught in each of those places the last time I fished them. I can also remember where hundreds of den and hickory trees are--where you can go and kill yourself a mess of squirrel any time you want. With a memory like this I have managed to remember enough things about my past that I am convinced that I was neither a pretty baby nor was I a good-looking kid. In fact I have been ugly my entire life. For instance the day Mom left Dr. Hopkins' Clinic with me, the first thing she did was cover my face with the burlap sack I was wrapped in. When I asked her about that many years later, she informed me the reason she did that was to keep the July sun out of my eyes but I have my doubts that was the reason. There are other reasons I am convinced that I was an ugly baby. As you know when a mother is showing her new baby to her friends, the first thing they do is reach down, pinch the newborn on the cheek, and remark, "How precious!" or say things like, "Isn't he cute?" In my case that did not happen. Nope! When they uncovered my face, Mom's friends would jerk their hands back as though they thought I was going to bite them or something. And instead of saying things like "How precious!" they would say "Gee, he sure has a big head!" or "I bet he can eat a lot." As time went on there were other things that would convince me that not only was I an ugly baby but I also was going to be an ugly kid. I remember when I was around five years of age Dad and I went to the sale barn in Popular Bluff, Missouri. On Fridays farmers would bring their livestock to the auction to sell. This particular time Dad was looking for a new milk cow. As we were walking along I spotted a pony. I remember it as though it were yesterday.

The horse was black and white with a black saddle and silver buckles. Now for a boy who rode stick horses, it was love at first sight. Not noticing I had stopped to look at the pony, Dad had gone on to see the livestock. When I realized this I went closer to get a better look at the pony. The man who owned it asked me if I would like to sit on the pony. When I answered "Yes," he offered me a deal. He told me if I would sit on the pony and play the little music box he handed me, I could stay all day. I soon learned the more I played the music box the more the people would gather around and give me peanuts and apples. Although I was separated from Dad, it turned into one of the best days of my life. As the day wore on fewer and fewer people were stopping by and the owner said he, too, had to go and suggested I find my dad. Getting down from the pony I gathered all the peanuts and apples I could carry and went looking for Dad. As the sun set I decided Dad must have left without me. So I found some bales of straw inside the barn to sleep on and settled in for the night. For the next several days I wandered around the sale barn petting the cows and horses that were still there, ate the apples and peanuts, and on occasion got some fresh milk from a couple of the milk cows. When the next Friday rolled around, I spotted Dad trying to buy a Thanksgiving turkey from one of the farmers. I quickly ran to Dad who was very happy to see me. We got the turkey and headed home together. Now don't misunderstand: both Dad and Mom had been very worried and had been looking for me. Indeed, Dad had made several trips back to Popular Bluff but somehow we kept missing each other. Mom had even made a deal with the local milkman. Hoping someone would recognize me, she persuaded him to allow her to paste my picture on the bottles of milk he was selling around the area. After a couple of days he told her he couldn't permit her to continue this practice anymore because he was losing too much business with my picture on the bottles. It took another twenty-five years for the idea to catch on of putting the pictures of missing children on milk cartons.

Now being an ugly kid did have its advantages. During the summer when we were not working in the fields, my sisters always had housework to do such as washing and ironing clothes, cleaning house, and other things that I didn't have to do. Mom always sent me to the garden to play her favorite game. She always wanted me to stand in the middle of the garden with my arms stretched out pretending I was flying (which I found to be a lot of fun). Of course, the benefit to Mom was that it kept the birds out of the garden. I remember one Halloween when I was probably seven or eight years old, Dad came up with the idea of not using a pumpkin as a jack-o-lantern. Instead he would use me. Dad took some planks off the porch and had me crawl under the porch and stick my head up through the hole. He put some pumpkin vines around me and placed candles on each side of my head and, sure enough, I looked a lot like a big jack-o-lantern. Only the bravest of the brave trick-or-treaters were courageous enough to come on the porch for candy. Therefore, we kids had extra candy for weeks. Now one would think being ugly would cause problems in school but it isn't as bad as you would think. After all I wasn't the only ugly kid in school. I had a friend who was so ugly his mother would have to put bacon pieces in his shirt pocket just to get the dog to play with him. One of the most embarrassing things that did happen was when it came time for school pictures to be taken, the photographer kept telling me to face the wall and not the camera. But James Shelton, the principal would always make the photographer retake my picture with me facing the right way. As I approached my early teens and junior high school, being ugly was less of an ordeal for me. Puberty was a big help. At this time, all the boys got gawky looking and were covered with acne; there wasn't a good looking boy in the bunch. However as we reached high school the other boys' complexions cleared up but I was still ugly. Once again, it kept me from reaching some of my goals in life. I took a drama class in high school which was one of the few classes I really liked. Mr. Bob Herring was the teacher and it was a great class. We had a lot of fun performing small plays for the school. After receiving only small roles, I asked Mr. Herring if I could have the starring role in our next play. Being the nice man he always was, he told me if we were to do "The Hunchback of Notre Dame" I could have the lead. Unfortunately the next play we performed was "The Valiant" and Jack Smith got the lead part. As you can see with all these facts you can understand why I have come to the conclusion that I was an ugly baby. The problem didn't get any better during my teens, but I have held tightly to the hope that sometime during my life I would be like the ugly duckling in the book Mom always read to me when I was young. I hoped that I, too, would someday turn into a swan. It hasn't occurred yet during my adult years. But my mother-in-law, Mazie—God rest her soul — would always tell me I was pretty. In fact she would say, "Jim, you are pretty three ways. You are <u>pretty</u> ugly and <u>pretty</u> apt to stay that way for a <u>pretty</u> long time."

However time does change all things. I am pushing sixty years of age and the wrinkles are beginning to cover some of the lumps on my face and my hair is turning a pretty color of white so I have high hopes of becoming a distinguished looking older man. If this doesn't work I have the promise of Ben Bradshaw, a friend of mine who is a mortician, that when my time has come and I pass from this earth, he can send me into the next world looking better than I do now.

Accepting the facts of life.

WHO DID IT

By: Terry Weldon

When I was about six and my sister, (Sissie) was about nine years old we were playing in the back yard. She would always try to get me to play with dolls, but I just couldn't bring myself to do it, even as a small boy. However, I could talk her into doing almost anything because she had no one else to play with.

We always started our day out excited to get outside and play. One day we were playing with cars in the back yard I had the great idea to build a tunnel for our cars to drive through. The ground in our yard was so hard, we couldn't scrape up enough dirt to build a hill big enough to make a tunnel through it.

We looked around for something to use and I ran across wicker clothes basket out by the clothes line in the back yard. It was perfect, but, Sissie said it was Granny's clothes basket for brining in the laundry from the clothesline. I told her we were just gonna borrow it for a while and we would put it back. We took it and it was perfect except for one thing, when we drove the cars into the tunnel, we couldn't reach them to get them out. I talked Sis into cutting the bottom out of the basket so we can access the cars from the top. When we finished playing, we placed the basket back by the clothesline and dropped the bottom we had cut out down in the basket. Once Granny gathered the clothes, filled the basket and went to pick it up, the bottom and all of her clothes hit the ground. Her response was, "Boy (which was my nickname), what have you done"? I jumped up from the ground and ran over to see what she was talking about. With the most surprised look on my face I could come up with, I confessed, "Sissie did it"!

A few days later Sis and I were playing around in the back yard where I had designed an excellent snare out of a piece of clothesline. We were using it for big game hunting in the chicken coop. I had it sticking through the chicken wire with the loop on the ground inside the coop. We had dropped some corn in the loop and were waiting for the big game to come by. Soon two big fat hens came over near us, scratching the ground and looking for food. They spotted the corn and both went after it, with each hen having a foot in the noose, I gave it a big jerk and low and behold, I caught both of them. With that, the two hens went crazy and began to squawk. It sounded like we were killing them. Granny came running out the back door yelling, "what on earth have you youngins' done now". With our backs to Granny, she couldn't see who was holding the clothesline snare, so I quickly handed it to Sis and wrapped it around her arm so she couldn't let go, jumped to my feet and shouted, "Sissie did it"!

She had avoided playing with me for a few days so I was in the backyard alone with a hand full of broom straws catching grub worms from the holes in our yard. How many of you have done that before? One of our favorite past times back then. Find those perfectly round holes in your yard, drop a broom straw (must be straight), into the hole and watch the grub worm start pushing it out of the hole. When he gets a good grip on the straw and is near the top of the hole, snatch on the straw and out he comes, excellent fishing bait. Anyway, I've got like three or four straws going at one time, I am slaying those rascals when Granny comes off the back porch screaming at me, "Boy, look what you have done now". She is carrying her best broom with a very large chunk of straws cut out of it. I knew I had used the old broom from the smoke house, cause I knew how mad Granny would get if I used her new broom, so I jumped to my feet in an attempt to explain my way out of this one when she showed me a note attached to the broom written by a small child that said, "Boy did it"! I saw sissie out of the corner of my eye hiding around the corner of the chicken house, snickering…

WHITE KNUCLES

By: Jim Ferguson

If you have fished or spent as much time on the water as I have you know Mother Nature can often deal you a bad hand every now and then. On more than one occasion I have had the experience of being caught on the water when Mother Nature showed her fury. Of all the times, there are three that really got my attention and I would like to share them with you. Number one, and probably the most dangerous of the three, occurred while I was fishing Donaldson Chute, a chute off the Mississippi River on the Tennessee side of the river. To reach it I would either put my boat into the Mississippi River at Marsh Landing near Bungee Corporation (east of Portageville) and travel upstream for a mile or more to Donaldson Chute or I would put in at Point Pleasant Chute, cross it into the river, and then cross over to the Tennessee side which is also more than a mile. On this particular day I had launched from Point Pleasant and had been fishing for the better part of the day and enjoying a great deal of success. Late that afternoon I noticed a dark cloud approaching from the west. As I watched it for a few minutes I also noticed that the wind was picking up. As I prepared to leave, I met a friend of mine motoring into the chute. As he approached me he asked how I was doing. I responded that I was limited out and, by the looks of the storm cloud that was approaching, I thought I would be heading back across the river before it got too bad. He said he thought it would probably swing south so he was going to stay and fish. As I neared the halfway point across the river, the wind really picked up and by the time I reached the boat ramp and got my boat loaded onto the trailer the storm hit. It hit with such a fury! Before I could get across the levy it was raining so hard I couldn't see to drive and the wind was strong enough that it blew the aluminum shell camper off the back of my truck and blew it across the field and totally destroyed it. The storm passed in a few minutes. As my thoughts returned to my buddy who was on the other side of the river, I decided to turn around and re-launch my boat in order to go check on him. Very shortly I heard him approaching the ramp. He looked like a drowned rat and had several inches of water in his boat. As we talked he told me he had decided to head back as well. He continued that when he was halfway across the river, he saw a tornado crossing over the river downstream a mile or so. He stated it was the worst he had ever seen the waves. He thanked me for staying around and checking on him. For years after that, whenever we ran into each other, we would always ask "Been across the river lately?"

The next story took place on Wappapello Lake where my brother-in-law, Toby Jordon, and I were fishing at the upper end of Lost Creek. Since it was the spring of the year and the crappie were spawning, we were catching some really nice fish. Considering it wasn't a very good day--it had been sprinkling all morning and looked as though it was going to come a down pour any minute--while we fished we were constantly listening to the thunder and watching the approaching cloud. As the storm came closer, we decided we had better head back when we realized we had waited too long. The storm hit and lighting was striking close. We decided to turn around and go back to where we were fishing. We had seen that someone had parked their truck on the shore. Beaching the boat we made a dash for the truck, climbed into the camper shell that was on it, and rode out the storm. It rained so hard we could not hear ourselves talk but we did manage to stay dry. After the storm passed we discovered our boat was half full of rain water but we were able to use the sump pump to drain it and we continued on with our days' fishing and caught our limit of fish which made a great memory. A few days later we returned with Lawrence Jordon, Toby's Dad. It was one of the few times I got to fish with him. We caught a lot of fish and he had a great time.

The third story I would like to tell you about also took place on the Mississippi River. I was fishing with my brothers-in-law: Lindel Cossey and Toby Jordon (if my memory serves me right it was Toby). We were fishing once again at Donaldson Chute and had launched our boat near Bungee at Marsh Landing just east of Portageville, Missouri. The day was sunny, the wind was calm, and it had all the appearance of a great day to be fishing. Although Toby and I had fished together for years and have shared many great memories together fishing and hunting, Lindel didn't get to go with us much because he was in the military. In fact he seldom went with us because Lindel is the type who would rather stay at home with a good book or engage in a conversation on an intellectual level. He and I were always doing that often driving the other members of the family nuts with our arguments ("debates" as we called them). Lindel always took the approach of facts and reasoning with me relying on BS to sustain my side of the argument. Lindel is a smart, educated man but he does have one flaw. He would, on occasion, have a memory lapse of the times he went fishing and hunting with me and the trouble we often experienced. Today would prove to be one of those lapses of memory. As the day proceeded along we once again caught a lot of fish, had a great time, and had a lot of laughs enjoying the day UNTIL Toby and I realized how hard the wind seemed to be blowing the tree tops. We decided the day was getting late and it was time to be going. As we approached the mouth of the chute entering the river we once again knew we had stayed too long. The Mississippi River was white capping which made the two mile trip back to the boat ramp both rough and dangerous. I gave Lindel a life jacket since he was not a swimmer. We took our positions in the boat: Toby sat on the front seat, Lindel sat on the Styrofoam cooler we were using to store fish, and I sat in the rear running the boat. We headed for the boat ramp. Not too far below the mouth of the chute there is a bend in the river where the water is always rough. With the wind blowing from the south like it was today, the waves were extremely high. Bursting through some of the waves, we took water over the front of the boat causing Lindel to come off the cooler. He then fell back down on the cooler causing to bust and leaving him sitting on the bottom of the boat in several inches of water with the fish floating around him. As he gripped the side of the boat trying to hang on, I noticed his knuckles were white from the death grip he had on the boat. I also saw the fear in his eyes. I will also admit to being concerned about making it back to the landing. But for whatever reason God blessed us and we made it back to the boat ramp safely. After loading the boat on the trailer and Lindel kissing the ground, we headed home with a good mess of fish and a great memory stored away for the future. As always time changes all things. Life goes on and new memories are made. If you know Lindel Cossey ask him to tell of this trip. It is one of his favorite stories. You might also ask him about learning to SKI--another adventure I may write about someday.

Thanks for the memories.

WILLIE

By: Jim Ferguson

I was born in 1952, and I'm sure the Fowlers heard of my arrival that day. They were family friends and would continue to be so for life. We lived northeast of Gideon at the end of Hartzel Lane while Mr. and Mrs. Fowler lived a little further east by a mile or so. Both families attended the Baptist Church in Tallapoosa together. Mr. and Mrs. Fowler had several children most of whom were older than I was by several years. Allen Ray was two years older and Freddy was one year younger and we often played baseball together. I spent many a night and Sunday afternoon at their home. There was Willie, too, who was several years older than I. Willie was what we refer to today as a child with special needs. Willie was severely handicapped and his speech was hard for a lot of people to understand but for us kids being raised with and around him, we had no problem. He also had other physical and mental problems. However, Mr. and Mrs. Fowler raised Willie as they did their other children. He had chores to do every day around the house and farm. Those chores were

Willie's life and he took them very seriously. He gathered the eggs from the hen house and shelled the corn and fed it to the chickens. Now Mr. Fowler had a corn-shelling device that would remove the corn from the cob, but Willie didn't like using it. Preferring to hand-shell it, he would sit for hours performing this very slow, tedious task. Willie took great pride in accomplishing this task and would fuss at us kids if we decided to give him a hand, telling us it was his job and promptly sending us on our way. He was always so protective of us, too. If he saw us doing something dangerous, he would often tell Mrs. Fowler. Now when Mrs. Fowler decided to have chicken for dinner, she would allow Alan, Freddy, and me to catch the chickens, ring their necks, and pluck them for her. Now for those of you who have never rung a chicken's neck, you have missed out on some really good fun. First you had to catch the chicken which was a chore in itself, but the real fun came once you caught it. Holding the chicken by the head, you would twirl it a few good spins until the head came off. Then you would just throw the chicken on the ground until it stopped flopping. That is where the phrase "running around like a chicken with its head off" came from. This scene was quite funny to watch especially when you were a young boy. Now I can tell you for a fact that Sunday dinner was always a great treat at Mrs. Fowler's table. She made the best green beans! I have a lot of memories of that house. The living room had varnished pine planks on the wall and I always thought it was so pretty. There was an old rocking chair in one corner with a cowhide stretched to make the seat and back. Another interesting thing about the inside of their house that I will never forget was the framed jigsaw puzzles hanging on the walls. In addition, there was always one in the process of being put together. The reason I'll never forget those puzzles is Willie would spend hours putting them together--huge puzzles. Some times they would take up the whole table. There were several hundreds or thousands of pieces in each of Willie's projects. I'd have <u>never</u> taken them on then nor would I today, but Willie (even with his poor eyesight) had a knack for them. Sadly, the house burned several years later and those puzzles were lost. Upon hearing of the fire, the puzzles were one of the first things that crossed my mind. After Mr. and Mrs. Fowler built a new home, Willie was once again putting his beloved puzzles together. Anther childhood memory I have of Willie is the days of riding bicycles. Upon reaching the normal age for riding a bike Alan, Freddy, and I learned to ride. Willie didn't learn to peddle his bike until his late teens, but he would straddle it and walk it as fast as we could ride. The day he did learn to peddle, you would have thought he hit the jackpot and, in a sense, he did. He was so excited! There was another day that wasn't nearly as exciting for Willie--the day he turned 18. His dad told him he would have to register for the draft. Having a brother who served in the military and also not completing understanding, Willie believed this meant he could be leaving home. So on the appointed day to go register, Willie went to the barn and hid.

And as always, time passes and changes all things. We three boys grew up. Allen went off to the army; Freddy moved away and married; I joined the Navy. Willie stayed at home with Mr. and Mrs. Fowler until their deaths several years later but not before having to go through the pain of losing Allen. Willie is now in a home and is quite happy according to the family members I've talked to throughout the last few years. I haven't seen him in fifteen years or so which is something I should do. I doubt if he would remember me but I sure remember him! I learned a lot growing up around Willie. It gave me the understanding and the knowledge that even though people with disabilities may be different, they still laugh, they still have talents, and they still love just like we do. We all have flaws and imperfections. Thanks for the memories, Willie.

In memory of Mr. and Mrs. Fowler and Allen.

LYLE'S LULLABY

By: Jim Ferguson

You remind me of someone I used to dream of.

You were just a twinkle in my eye.

But now you lay your head upon my shoulder

And I watch you as you slowly close your eyes.

Go to sleep little boy; dream of puppy dogs.

Go to sleep little boy; dream of catching frogs.

Run through the valleys and over the hills

To the meadows that wait for you on the other side.

Run on and play, my son, 'til this day is done

Then come back to your daddy's side.

And some day, when you are older

And have a boy of your own,

You'll know the joys I've known in having a son.

Go to sleep little boy; dream of puppy dogs.

Go to sleep little boy; dream of catching frogs.

For the nighttime's made for sleeping and

Tomorrow there'll be time to play.

So what do you say? Let's go to sleep, little boy.

Go to sleep little boy; go to sleep.

NOTE: I wrote this song for my infant son, Lyle. We lost him at the age of 21 in February, 1998. Although he never got to know the joy of having his own children, Lyle loved little children very much.

Made in the USA
Charleston, SC
01 December 2012